JUN 2 1 1996

World-Class
New Product
Development

Benchmarking
Best Practices of
Agile Manufacturers

Dan Dimancescu & Kemp Dwenger

amacom
American Management Association
New York • Atlanta • Boston • Chicago • Kansas City • San Francisco • Washington, D.C.
Brussels • Mexico City • Tokyo • Toronto

This publication is designed to provide accurate and authoritative
information in regard to the subject matter covered. It is sold with the
understanding that the publisher is not engaged in rendering legal,
accounting, or other professional service. If legal advice or other expert
assistance is required, the services of a competent professional person
should be sought.

Library of Congress Cataloging-in-Publication Data

Dimancescu, Dan.
    World-class new product development : benchmarking best practices
of agile manufacturers / Dan Dimancescu and Kemp Dwenger.
        p.   cm.
    Includes bibliographical references and index.
    ISBN 0-8144-0311-5
    1. New products—Management.   2. Production management.
3. Benchmarking (Management)   I. Dwenger, Kemp. II. Title.
    HF5415.153.D56   1996
    658.5'75—dc20   95-25611
                                                                CIP

Printing number

10   9   8   7   6   5   4   3   2   1

Contents

Preface   vii

Acknowledgments   xv
- The IAPD Strawman Model • A Book for Managers
- Our Objective

Part One   **1**

1   **Inside the Do Loop**   **3**
- Why Things Go Wrong • Common Problems Across Companies

2   **Managing the Whole**   **18**
- A New System of Management • A Three-Tier Enabling Hierarchy • Old Ways Die Hard • Crafting a New Understanding

3   **The Product Development Process**   **38**
- The Widening Span of Team Accountability
- Control Over Decisions • Seamless Communication and Information Sharing

Part Two   **55**

4   **Best Practices**   **57**

5   **Strategic Process Teaming**   **61**
- Understanding Teaming • Important Teaming Characteristics

6   **Four-Fields Process Mapping**   **80**
    • A Tiered Mapping Process   • Four-Fields Applications

7   **A System of Metrics**   **91**
    • Three Types of Metrics   • Limitations of Metrics

8   **Reviews**   **106**
    • A Tool Kit of Review Methods   • Applying the Review
    Methods

9   **Product Definition**   **119**
    • Product Definition   • Quality Function
    Deployment   • Translating the Voice of the Customer
    Into Products   • Conclusion

10 **Technology Management**   **140**
    • A Three-Track R&D Continuum
    • R&D Strategy vs. Business Strategy   • Identifying Core
    Technologies   • Bottleneck Engineering   • Organizational
    Links

11 **Suppliers as Partners**   **152**
    • Japan's Innovation: Vertical Aggregation
    • The Silicon Valley Innovation: Vertical Disaggregation
    • The Welsh Hybrid: A Shared Learning Network
    • Supplier Partnerships

12 **Rewards and Recognition**   **165**

13 **Knowledge Management**   **173**

Part Three   **185**

14 **Continuous Change**   **187**
    • The New Organization   • Change and Product Development

15 **Ten X**   **194**

Appendix A: New Organizational Models and Trends   **199**
    • The Information Processing Model
    • New Organizational Forms   • Network
    Organizations   • Macrolevel Network Forms

Appendix B: Enabling Hierarchies **212**

Appendix C: Toshiba's Research and Development
Organization **220**

Appendix D: Supplier Relationships in Japan: Case Studies **224**
  • Yokogawa-Hewlett-Packard, Ltd. (YHP) • Alps

Appendix E: NEC: A Commitment to Change **228**

Index **231**

Preface

The inception of this book goes back to 1987 when Cary Kimmel of the Xerox Corporation had just concluded a benchmarking study of leading U.S. manufacturers of industrial and commercial electronics equipment without uncovering any evidence of a replicable body of best practices. Rather, all the companies in the study shared similar frustrations and a belief that order-of-magnitude improvements were needed in moving products from the conceptual stage into the hands of customers. That year, he asked InterMatrix, a London-based consulting firm of which Kemp Dwenger is a U.S.-based principal, to benchmark the product development process of ten leading European-based electronics firms.

The subsequent comparison of European firms in 1988 produced a similar conclusion: no best practices and many similar problems. The number one problem on everyone's list of unresolved issues was *communication across organizational boundaries.* When this was mentioned to a respected management guru some years later, his response was, "So what's new? We've known that for twenty-five years!" He was right; there was nothing new in the finding.

Indeed, one of the most perceptive studies of business performance was written early in the 1960s. It characterized companies as mechanistic and organic, definitions that 30 years later closely align with our own two types. At that time, communication was already seen as a significant problem:

> Information required for the proper functioning of the organization is not passed from person to person in accordance with the needs issuing from the tasks to be performed, but

is used—or is thought to be used—to demonstrate superior worth or status.

Information, in fact, may become an instrument for advancing, attacking, or defending status. A production meeting was called in one concern to discuss the layout of a new production line requiring special methods. The meeting began with the layouts which had been prepared by a planning engineer (in his evenings). Questions were raised about them and discussion went on for some 15 minutes. The chairman, the Works Manager, then announced that the layout would, in any case, have to be drastically altered, and the usable space curtailed.

There was a brief silence. When was this decided? At a meeting of top management on Tuesday (three days before). After a further pause the chairman went on to propose an alternative layout. Discussion began about the production methods to be used.

Afterwards, the planning engineer who had done the preparatory work said, "It's a bloody waste of time."[1]

Communication problems are traced in large part to an organizational legacy that fragmented companies into less and less cooperative parts. As a result, there is no hope of achieving the effective cross-boundary communication that is so essential to managing complex processes such as product development without extraordinary effort or by going around the system. Old ways don't work, so ad hoc new ones are created and patched on.

In 1990 the original benchmarking effort took a significant turn, thanks to Arnoud de Meyer, at France's noted INSEAD business school in Fontainebleau. Long a student of Japanese management practices in product development, his research underscored the importance of a body of robust and well-honed practices in *product development*, particularly in the electronics and automotive industries. These, he suggested, were much more than the already widely publicized quality control techniques. Indeed, they constituted a whole new dimension to the management of complex organizational issues such as one would encounter in product development.

Similar impressions were surfacing, too, through the extensive research of Michael Cusumano at MIT and Kim B. Clark, Robert H. Hayes, Takahiro Fujimoto, David Garvin, and Steven C. Wheelwright at Harvard.[2] At the same time, the publication of *The Machine That Changed the World* by a collegium of scholars helped focus a large business audience on the need for a radical turn in how large companies might better manage their affairs.[3]

But how this was to be achieved in day-to-day terms remained elusive—and frustrating to Kemp Dwenger, who led the European benchmarking effort for Xerox and brought a line executive's perspective to the problem. He had retired as senior vice president of GTE International with responsibilities during that period that included two joint ventures in Japan. One of these was with NEC and another with a family-owned enterprise. He had already concluded that their best quality practices, many of which originated in the United States, were indeed identifiable and transferable to Western firms. In other words, they were not simply a unique manifestation of Japanese culture. What was needed was a deeper firsthand analysis of what Arnoud de Meyer had observed.

To take a next step, he teamed up with Dan Dimancescu, president of TSG and a guest faculty member at Dartmouth College's Thayer School of Engineering. Long an observer of Japanese management, Dimancescu had convened a series of pioneering colloquia on Japanese cross-function management methods for a group of Fortune 500 executives. Held at the Thayer School in Hanover, New Hampshire, in 1988, and subsequently in 1990 and 1993, the purpose was to tackle the *how-to* that had to date eluded reports of Japanese successes in product development, particularly in the automotive and electronics sectors that had captured Arnoud de Meyer's attention. The first colloquium highlighted the significance of U.S. management experiments in product development such as Ford's successful *Team Taurus*, widely credited with turning the company's fortunes around when the new car line was introduced in 1986. Lewis Veraldi, the team leader, brought a revealing insight in his presentations at the Dartmouth conference. One was a novel organization chart that abandoned the pyramid motif in favor of a circular pattern, with Lew at the middle. "Everyone can talk to anyone else directly on this chart. There are no communication barriers."[4] Lew would fight that battle hard against functional barons holding firm to their barriers.

From visits over many years to major Japanese manufacturing firms and discussions with quality experts in Japan, Dimancescu concluded that a key to their success was not just the disciplined attention to total quality but also a new class of horizontal processes. Seen as a genuine step-change in management practice, developed at Toyota and Komatsu during the early 1960s, these were widely deployed throughout major Japanese firms. Product development was one of those new horizontal processes.[5] They offered a strong foundation through which to manage businesses systematically.

These horizontal processes had four unique characteristics not yet present in mainstream U.S. management:

1. They were designed to achieve *company-wide cross-department cooperation and communication.*
2. They focused on a few key *strategic core processes* as a basis for achieving competitive results and profitability.
3. They were *team managed by line people closest to the process.*
4. They were not culturally idiosyncratic and thus were *potentially transferable practices.*

Significantly, there was nothing akin to these horizontal processes in the Western management tool kit. Even after 30 years of evolution in Japan, they remained largely unstudied and unreported and hence unnoticed in Western academic and business literature. It was not until 1988 that the first Japanese book containing a score of cross-function case studies appeared. Although immediately translated by the author with support from Digital, it took five years for it to be published in English. Even then it achieved only a small circulation in the United States and next to none in Europe.[6]

The how-to insights into cross-function management that Dimancescu gained complemented the direction taken by the initial Xerox/InterMatrix benchmarking study. The two activities were merged in 1990 into a new organization, the International Association for Product Development (IAPD). A collaborative research effort, over the next five years it gained the support and active involvement of 33 Fortune 500 firms from the United States, Europe, and Japan.[7]

The IAPD Strawman Model

At the request of its members, the IAPD built a high-level straw-man model of Japanese management that highlighted two main characteristics: (1) the role of strategic cross-company processes as an *organizational* breakthrough of global importance and (2) the importance of horizontal communication and information sharing across organizational boundaries as the critical *operational* feature of those processes. This model became a lens through which to compare and to benchmark practices.

In this manner a growing list of best practices in Japan, the United States, and Europe was identified. One by one, these were detailed during an ongoing series of quarterly workshops by executives and managers of member and nonmember firms as well as academics and consultants. In many cases, presentations to the IAPD did not meet the best-practice test because they failed to demonstrate significant benefit or that they were indeed replicable.

In time, a picture of product development as a whole system of methods and practices evolved. It is built on a practical premise that process management can itself be the strategy, and from it came our use of the phrase *strategic process management* as a description. In other words, competitive advantage had become as much a matter of superior process management as of leveraging capital, skilled people, and core technology.

A Book for Managers

Part One of the book provides a general overview of product development and the central organizational issues that large firms have faced in the 1990s. The words *horizontal* and *strategic process* are used to paint a picture of a new management style breaking away from Tayloristic legacies. This transition was expressed in unmistakably clear terms in July 1993 when *Business-Week* featured the Harvard Business School on the cover with the subtitle, "Is it outmoded?"

Part Two describes a tool kit of best practices being applied by world-class companies to the management of the product development process. Although the practices described are elements of a single, unified management system, the chapters can be read independently of one another.

In Part Three, we close with a discussion about continuous change and the need for a systemic approach to the managing of large, complex organizations.

OUR OBJECTIVE

An underlying theme to this book is the importance of a systemic approach to the management of complex organizations in meeting world-class competitive standards. One of our objectives has been to characterize what this means and how it is achieved in creating successful new products. Although many of our examples are taken from manufacturing companies, the insights are of direct and immediate value to individuals in other industries, including services.

Throughout we have highlighted key thoughts to provide a shortcut to ideas. This book is a work in progress. It is now evident that the Western corporate learning curve, implementing a process-driven competitive strategy, is steep and accelerating; all signs point to a continued and rapid ascent.

Don Dimancescu
TSG—8 Story Street
Cambridge, Massachusetts 02138
Tel. 617-494-1111; Fax 617-547-2378
e-mail: tsg@std.world.com

Kemp Dwenger
InterMatrix, Inc.
10 Corbin Drive
Darien, Connecticut 06820
Tel. 203-662-1000; Fax 203-655-3130

Notes

1. Tom Burns and G. M. Stalker, *The Management of Innovation* (London: Tavistock Publications, 1994), p. 152.

2. Michael Cusumano, *The Japanese Automobile Industry* (Cambridge: Harvard University Press, 1985) and *Japan's Software Factories* (New York: Oxford University Press, 1991).

3. J. Womack, D. Jones, and D. Roos, *The Machine That Changed the World* (New York: Rawson Associates, 1990).

4. See excellent Taurus case study written by Professor James Brian Quinn and Penny Paquette at the Amos Tuck School of Business, Dartmouth College, 1990.

5. See Dan Dimancescu, *The Seamless Enterprise: Making Cross-Functional Management Work* (New York: Harper/Business, 1992).

6. Kenji Kurogane, ed., *Cross-Functional Management: Principles and Practical Applications* (Tokyo: Asia Productivity Organization, 1993).

7. The companies benchmarked were Alps, Brother, Canon, CSK, Enplan, Fuji Xerox, Fujitsu, Hitachi, Ichiko, Intec, Japan Research Development Corp., Juki, Kobayashi Kose, Koito, Komatsu, NEC, NEC-NIMS, Nissan, Philip NKO Group, Sony, Stanley, TKD, Toko, Toshiba, Toyota, and Yokogawa-Hewlett-Packard.

Acknowledgments

Our thanks go to the many individuals, executives, consultants, and academics who participated in various meetings of the International Association for Product Development (IAPD) and openly shared their know-how. The IAPD member companies between 1990 and 1995 were: ABB, Abbott Labs, Allied Signal, Apple, ATT (Bell Labs), Bay Networks (originally named SynOptics), BT plc (British Telecom), Digital, Dow Chemical, DuPont Electronics (renamed Berg), Eastman Kodak, General Electric Medical Systems, Hewlett-Packard, Honeywell, IBM, Intel, Landis & Gyr, Loctite, National Semiconductor, NCR, Northern Telecom, Philips, Pitney Bowes, Rockwell International, Sony, Sun Microsystems, Texas Instruments, Textron, Trane, Westinghouse, the Welsh Development Agency (representing Calsonic, Hills, Mitel, Pilkington Optronics, Rexham, TRW, and Trico), and Xerox. And to the many others with whom we have shared conversations at their work sites in the United States, Japan, and Europe. Thanks go as well to Virginia Phostole at InterMatrix and Ned Parsons at TSG, whose administrative efforts have helped to make the IAPD so effective an organization, and to Frank Basa, who as a Ph.D. candidate at MIT's Sloan School, helped research topics and track subjects.

In Japan, for their help and cooperation, we thank Professor Seiichiro Yonakura of Hitotsubashi University, Professor Teruo Yamanouchi of Daitobunka University, Dr. Genya Chiba of the Research and Development Corporation of Japan, members of the Japan Union of Scientists and Engineers, and finally the many companies that over the years have been open and candid in sharing their experiences. Of these, NEC was of particular help, given one of the author's long-standing association with the firm through joint venture relations.

We are particularly indebted to Charles Hutchinson, who retired in 1994 as dean of the Thayer School of Engineering at Dartmouth College, for his sponsorship of several conferences in Hanover, New Hampshire, on new management ideas between 1988 and 1993. We thank Yves Thomas, who, as director of IRESTE and more recently as managing director of Atlantech in Nantes, France, offered to host a meeting of U.S. and French leading thinkers in new organizational concepts under the auspices of the Institut de l'Homme et la Technologie at the Abbaye de Villeneuve in 1994.

In crafting this manuscript, we are indebted to our editor, Anthony Vlamis at AMACOM books, for having taken the risk on an unvarnished version of this book. Thanks to the skilled treatment by Roberta Tovey in Belmont, Massachusetts, our manuscript became a finished product. It would otherwise have been unreadable.

And to our families for bearing with the ubiquitous laptops and late hours, we are most grateful.

PART ONE

The lateral organization increases the capacity of the entire organization to make more decisions more often. . . .
Lateral organizations create an ability to be multidimensional and flexible. . . . By combining decision making and implementation in the same roles, the motivation of the implementers is increased.

Jay Galbraith, *Competing With Flexible Lateral Organizations*

Chapter 1
Inside the Do Loop

During the Korean War, U.S. pilots flew into combat with aircraft that were less powerful than the acclaimed MIG fighters. The F-86 did have one key advantage, however. It was far more maneuverable. A pilot ahead of an approaching MIG could loop back on it before the enemy could itself loop around. This was known as "getting inside the do loop."

Two kinds of companies inhabit today's business world: those trying to win through rigid hierarchical control in which orders are tightly executed from the top down and those trying to win by building lean and flexible organizations that can adapt to rapid change and greater complexity. As the former are finding themselves less and less able to compete, the latter have mastered a fundamental do-loop principle: They win by achieving fast delivery cycles and offering more value at less cost to their customers. How do they do it?

To find out, we spent more than six years gauging the management practices at almost 100 technology-intensive companies in the United States, Japan, and Europe. Our best examples come from companies with fast cycle times, rapid market share gains, high percentages of sales from products introduced within the past three years, and strong customer images. From them emerges an innovative style of management built on a new awareness of cross-organization processes as a systemic solution to the complexity they face. Product development is one of these.

One thing is sure, however: Success in product development is not easy. It takes fortitude, vision, and teamwork to achieve and retain world-class performance standards. "Overall," observed *BusinessWeek*, using particularly graphic terms, "the new-product battleground is a scene of awful carnage. . . . Of 11,000 new products launched by 77 manufacturing, service, and consumer-product companies, [only] a little more than half were still on the market five years later." For those that are succeeding in this unforgiving environment, it means speed in managing a full product development cycle within the cycle time of a competitor—in other words, getting inside the competitor's do loop—and gaining as deep an understanding of customers as possible in order to maximize the odds of market acceptance.

Japanese firms such as Toyota, Honda, and Sony did just this in the 1970s and 1980s, most visibly in the automotive, motorcycle, and electronics industries. During those decades, North American customers voted by the tens of millions, and as a result, many brand-name U.S. corporations such as Ford and Xerox were pushed to the wall. The effects were so debilitating that American firms had to change their ways or go out of business. Many, including century-old brand names in the machine tool industry, vanished from the scene. Yet others accepted the challenge and aggressively went about transforming the way they do business. Within a decade, however, Japanese best practices in product development had spread rapidly into Western firms, and a whole new cycle of innovative management experiments took root.

> The challenge is to get a full product development cycle within the cycle time of a competitor and to do it with maximum odds of acceptance by the marketplace.

The learning in many cases has been rapid. By 1990, Boeing Commercial Aircraft faced a tough competitor, Airbus, which was rapidly eating away at its market share and profitability. To recover lost ground, Boeing leaders knew they would have to change the way in which design engineers worked in compartmentalized disciplines and assembly people functioned in a separate world from the designers. By not treating the development of new aircraft as a systemic process, the company suffered costly inefficiencies in the design and production processes.

In a bold move, a wholly new way of design—working and responding to customer needs—was instituted with the launching of the 777 aircraft program. Old ways were jettisoned and new ones swiftly instituted. When one of us worked with Boeing's 777 aircraft 14-person pilot design-build team, called Section 41, colocation of design and assembly teams was still a novelty, as was the use of a fully integrated, online, three-dimensional system for designing the whole aircraft electronically. Not ten months later, however, almost 10,000 designers from more than 200 teams filtered through an intensive training program that brought them up to speed in the new ways in which teaming and design work would occur.

Four years later, the experiment proved successful. In April 1994, when the first 777 test aircraft throttled itself successfully aloft, a senior manager spoke with unabashed enthusiasm of his company's achievement: "We didn't know whether we had succeeded or not in our goal of having parts simply snap together the first time on the assembly floor. But they did. We put on a cargo door and 'bam'—it fit." This perfect coordination had never happened just right before; now, it would save the company money, time, frustration, and frayed nerves. More important, it would help them attack the Airbus challenge head-on. The 777-200B aircraft was designed to be as cost-effective to fly as the A340-300X Airbus but providing 30 more seats. Thus, on a cost-per-mile basis, it would offer a much better return to an airline. The results got even better. In May 1995, the Federal Aviation Administration announced that Boeing could skip the usual two-year testing phase because its aircraft was so well conceived in design and passed early cross-ocean tests so effectively. This decision bought the company an opportunity to accelerate at least several billion dollars in earlier revenue and gain another leg up on its competition. Such improvements are familiarly called $5\times$ or $10\times$ in scale because they bring dramatic and beneficial changes into effect.

NEC-NIMs, which designs integrated chips for its parent

company, NEC, is another company that learned to move from a design concept to a customer-desired solution flawlessly. In 1980 when NIMS was founded, only 18 percent of its integrated chips were designed right the first time. Eight out of ten times the design team had to get back to work because the solution it submitted either did not work or did not meet the requirements. By 1987, after a steady pace of internal improvements, the same firm was submitting design samples to its client and getting them right the first time at a 98.9 rate—and within schedule. This, too, exemplified a $5\times$ to $10\times$ improvement capability.

Most firms are not this good. Surveying a broad cross-section of product development efforts, a consulting company found that "47 percent of all product development work is repeated, due to upstream changes or late consideration of requirements; a full 51 percent of product development activity consists of fire-fighting, or unplanned activities; project hand-offs are often botched because of poor communication." These are dramatic revelations, particularly considering the direct cost and the lost opportunity measured in unbooked sales.

Stories such as these are one reason that the International Association for Product Development (IAPD), a consortium of world-class companies, came into being in 1990. The members shared similar war stories in product development. One of the members calls them "black eyes." Another member, a sophisticated maker of electronic testing instruments, estimated that a two-year delay in developing one instrument, caused by managerial inertia and inefficiency, lost the company between $300 and $700 million in potential revenues. Ironically, these are premier companies with respected products in the global market, yet each acknowledged ample room for improvement. Targeted performance improvement rates of 50 percent or more by even the best companies are viewed as essential just to stay competitive.

Why Things Go Wrong

Based on numerous diagnoses of these companies' product development processes, we came to recognize several widely shared problems, illustrated in the following examples.

Case One: Saab Car Still Has Bugs

"Saab Automotive AB has acknowledged that one of its car models was rife with defects last year and still needs improvement. . . . [These problems were acknowledged] after a corporate video labeled 'for internal use only' was disclosed by news organizations here. . . . Among customer complaints [in the redesigned 900 model] are brakes prone to weakening when wet and extraordinarily poor floor heating, a particularly curious defect in a country that is known for its bitter winters. . . . Saab's chief spokesman, Torsten Aman, [is quoted] as saying he had never before witnessed so many problems with a new model. Peter Moeller, head of technical development and production for the company, explained that 'we were extremely pressed when we developed this model.' The urgency to get out a new model had not allowed enough time to cope with the defects."[1]

Case Two: Findings From a Diagnosis of a Company's Product Development Process

This case, which we carried out at a company site, focused on the development of electronic controls for chemical processing plants worldwide. The solution was designed by a systems integrator firm in partnership with external vendors of computers and software. Our debriefing of 12 development team members uncovered a long list of issues not uncommon in many other industries.

What was not working as well as it might?

- The hardware decision was made before a software solution was devised. The software had to adapt to it. This caused delays.
- The hardware-software solution was suboptimal because it was not as fluid as it should have been.
- Corporate technology offices dictated a solution contrary to the development team's advice.
- During initial testing, the company and its lead hardware supplier did not resolve problems easily.
- Core team members had trouble working directly and com-

municating with the customers—in this case, the processing plants.
- Because of overly optimistic expectations at interim points, things were tested too early.
- The company team and the key hardware partner used completely different software problem report methods and operated at two different sites. E-mail and file transfers were the patchwork link.
- The hardware partner underestimated the equipment needs.
- The team and its partners focused not on a total system design but on subparts that eventually required redesigning for them to function as a system.
- Closer to the deadline, systems integration became an issue as component versions changed.
- The team and its partners did not have joint reviews.

The diagnostic vignette in Case Two is far from unique. It describes circumstances that are far more common than not across a wide band of companies in varied industries.

- Poor communication
- Solutions dictated from above
- Inadequate understanding of the customer
- Inefficient management of the process
- Divergent expectations

We have grouped these problems into six categories, although these are not meant to be exhaustive.

Common Problems Across Companies

One: Customer Needs Not Well Defined or Understood

The most pervasive problem, we discovered, happens early in the product development cycle when customer requirements are determined. This finding was confirmed by a thorough internal study at Hewlett-Packard carried out by a senior manager, Edith Wilson, in 1989 and 1990. "Why did some projects succeed in gaining market share profitably and others not?" she wanted to know.[2] After interviewing development teams on 19 projects, she concluded that a single factor dominated all others in determining the success or failure of a project.

> In seven out of ten failure cases, users' needs were not carefully gathered by the development team. This kind of lapse leads inexorably to the wrong designs and lackluster market acceptance.

In seven out of ten failure cases, Wilson found, users' needs were not carefully gathered by the development team. This kind of lapse leads inexorably to the wrong designs and lackluster market acceptance. In one case a large electronics company developed a brilliant sound system for PCs. But no one had bothered to test the whole system in actual use. If they had, they would have found that the sound system was so acoustically pure and strong that it caused the computer screen to blur. Problems of this sort were so widespread, we concluded, that the biggest opportunity for a breakthrough in Western companies' product development practices was in mastering the front end of the product development cycle, the period during which user needs are sought and specified. It was already evident that Japanese firms in several industries succeeded in large part because of a disciplined—albeit almost pedantic—effort to clarify user needs. Through well-structured analyses, they developed methods of determining not only explicitly stated but also latent needs. The state of the art has since moved back to the United States.

Two: Errors Found Too Late

Our homework confirmed as well what many other observers had started to note as a Western weakness: excessively high errors throughout the development cycle, causing costly rework and often the loss of customer goodwill. High error rates were especially common in organizations that still favored serialized development of the product development process. In such cases work is fragmented into pieces that mirror departmental or functional turf. The modus operandi is invariably adversarial; mistakes are not caught but passed on, and someone else is always to blame. In such an environment, protecting one's flanks is important. Nobody really likes it, but that is how it works in many companies.

Errors often result, too, from undisciplined reviews at critical decision points. In a departmentalized organization, individuals reviewed only what they were held responsible for; no one took responsibility for the whole endeavor, so errors migrated closer and closer to the finish line, forcing costlier corrections to be made with greater and greater frenzy as production deadlines drew near. Boeing managers calculated that before the 777 aircraft project, design changes and errors cost the company almost 33 percent of the total labor on a development program.[3] "One engineer out of three exists to fix mistakes made by the other two," stated Phil Condit, then general manager of the 777 Division, in a televised address to employees. This may work when the competition is weak and cash is available. It doesn't when profit margins get tight, and competitors are biting away at market share.

Another reason for errors is a "we can do anything" engineering attitude that often allows the development of untested technology during the product development cycle, even if such technology is intended as a central feature of a new product. The newly developed technology that has not been proved in actual use—meaning its robustness is not proved—can lead to breakdowns when a whole system is tested or the product is first put into commercial service. A famous example is the ill-fated smokeless cigarette. When demonstrated in a much-publicized press conference, the cigarette failed to light up. With that fiasco went several hundred million dollars into oblivion. Many times the first one to find out about these problems is the customer—*after* having invested in the purchase of the product.

> The best companies have a design error curve that peaks early with few, if any, errors occurring at the time of production.

Errors that occur late in the process bring about crisis management, with skilled staff cannibalized from other projects to complete this project, thus sacrificing other priorities. Instead, design change orders and error rates should be controlled so that they peak very early in the product development cycle; engineering effort will also peak early, and the project will reach conclusion far sooner than otherwise. Companies that achieve this level of effectiveness can assign skilled and scarce engineers to new project development teams even before the first project is finished. By managing the error and engineering effort curves to peak as early as possible, companies can develop overlapping project cycles. This is what the best do-loopers do: start the next project before the first one is finished, in the process reducing the time to market substantially. Overlapping project cycles allows companies such as Chrysler (cars), Compaq (laptops), and Cyrix (computer chips) to beat the competition by getting into their competitors' do loops. It is a winning strategy.

Cyrix, a privately held company founded in 1988, decided to go after Intel's computer chip markets by the do-loop method. "If we do 18-month design cycles," says Kevin McDonough, the company's engineering vice president, "and they do 3- to 4-year design cycles, we are going to get there before them."[4] At Cyrix, development cycles overlap in such a way that there is only a 6- to 12-month gap between new-product introductions. This cycle has not gone unnoticed at Intel (see Exhibit 1-1). A four-year gap separated the release of Intel's 486 and the 586 chips; a two-year gap separated the 586 from the next introduction; only six months lapsed between Intel's following generations in 1995. However, Cyrix's 686 development time line was projected as a do-loop falling within the longer Intel development time line. Of course, "it's always easier to imitate something than to create the original," says Intel vice president Paul S. Otellini of his competitor. However, similar strategies allowed the Japanese electronics and auto industries to pull the rug out from under their U.S. and European competitors.

Three: Management by Interference

Micromanagement is the worst of enemies, especially to a dedicated product development team. Teams are held on a short de-

Exhibit 1-1. Development cycles at Cyrix and Intel.

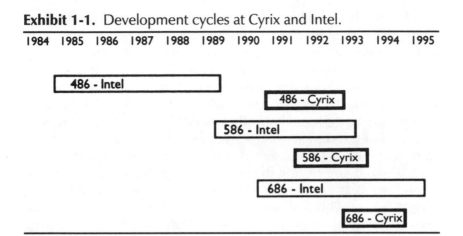

| 1984 | 1985 | 1986 | 1987 | 1988 | 1989 | 1990 | 1991 | 1992 | 1993 | 1994 | 1995 |

cision-making leash and often are given no warning of fundamental shifts in priority. In some companies, budgetary decisions are made annually by the senior management team. This may sound like good and tough management, but it is demoralizing for product development teams working on two- or three-year programs. They are kept in limbo at each annual budget review, wondering whether they will receive funding. Inevitably work slowly grinds to a halt as the team waits for a decision. Continuity suffers, as does any intelligent ability to forecast expectations.

Management by interference may have worked in rigid, heavily bureaucratic organizations, but it does not where there are far more outsourcing partners and a demanding customer environment. When the pressure is on, the senior manager no longer has the ability or the skill for direct day-to-day control of direct reports. Too much is happening, too fast, beyond his or her scope of attention. Crisis management as a way of doing business becomes the problem, not the solution. If, instead, teams are sure that their decisions will be honored and supported, projects can be managed with greater flexibility and speed.

Four: Too Many Projects

"We just don't seem to be able to get projects completed on time" is a common refrain. So is the lament, "Our people are spread too thin; we cannot plan resource usage because they are always busy solving some last-minute problem." Comments such as these are heard in the best of companies. In a Welsh-based subsidiary of an American firm, a product development staff of 40 people were responsible in 1994 for almost 140 projects. "Nothing is getting done as well as we would like," reflected the managing director. When asked whether each project carried equal weight and, if not, how projects were weighted, he answered, "We have no method of weighting the merits of one against another." In such a situation, and it is a common one, management has failed to build a system that works. Unable to prioritize, everything, profitable or not, passes through the door.

> Project overload is one of the first symptoms of senior management abdication of its responsibility.

Project overload is one of the first symptoms of senior management abdication of responsibility. Yet if fast and effective time to market is the goal, management should be investing its effort and analytical capacity in setting priorities. The Welsh subsidiary found this out. By developing a more rigorous filtering procedure for new projects, it immediately pared its priority list down from 140 to 35 key projects. Within weeks, projects were moving faster to conclusion, opening the door to another round of prioritized projects.

At one large global corporation, ten members of a development team were queried on their time commitments to this particular project and the commitments shared over other programs and projects at any one time. These are the findings:

Team Member	Percentage of Time on Project	Total Commitments
Leader	85	2 projects
Marketing	30	2 programs
Marketing	10	N.A.

(continues)

Team Member	Percentage of Time on Project	Total Commitments
Business manager	25	2 programs and 3 projects
Materials/parts	30	10–12 projects
Supplier chain	100	1 project
Materials management	20	6–7 products
Materials engineer	25	4–5 projects
Business analyst	20	2 products
Service engineer	100	1 project

This is not an easy environment in which to do one's best or to sustain focus. There is too much pulling most of these people in too many directions. Besides, it leaves too much to the question: Which boss's priority do I really serve?

Five: Burnout

The best-selling book *The Soul of a New Machine* by Tracy Kidder is many years old (it was published in 1981), but the tale it relates is still relevant. Kidder details the labors of a product development team at Data General, a Boston-area maker of minicomputers. Working under tight deadlines, a team of developers with a hard-driven leader struggled over months through a string of long days and long nights to achieve the impossible. The story, which most people read as another American high-tech success story, is really just the opposite. The team did indeed create the new wiz-bang machine, but the effort took its toll; the team disbanded, and individuals on it left the company disenchanted. Burnout had hit them. The individuals lost the zeal that might have been channeled into the next breakthrough, and the company lost excellent and dedicated workers.

The learning this team experienced was neither recorded nor passed on; knowledge accumulated at great personal and company cost simply dissipated.

This example does not exemplify best practice. The learning this team experienced was neither recorded nor passed on; knowledge accumulated at great personal and company cost simply dissipated. Also, it would take time and considerable good fortune for the company to ramp itself up to the next team effort, especially a successful one.

Almost every company can describe teams of this sort. They may be given exotic names, such as SWAT or TIGER teams. They usually excel because they are focused, well led, and driven to succeed. Yet many of them burn out and with them goes valuable competitive knowledge. A fallow period follows.

Six: Poor Communication

It happens all the time: A team comes together at a critical moment, let's say for a review. Someone makes a status report. A discussion ensues, and then comes the expected remark: "Well, I never knew that you meant to go in this direction. It just wasn't communicated." In short, no one bothered to brief all the team members or to reach consensus on the basics: terminology, requirements, goals, or review criteria.

"There is a law of optimum size of organizations," writes system theorist Ludwig von Bertalanffy. "The larger the organization grows, the longer is the way of communication and this, depending on the nature of organizations, acts as the limiting factor."[5] Indeed, a survey of large companies reported in May 1994 by *BusinessWeek* indicated that of the employees polled, 64 percent do not believe what management says, 61 percent are not well informed of company plans, and 54 percent do not get decisions explained well.

In many cases, the top echelons fail to communicate. They never explain strategy or clarify their rationale or constraints for an initiative. Teams are thus left in the dark and invariably second-guessed when it comes to critical decisions. This demoralizing and debilitating problem gets worse the deeper one probes. One example is the gathering of user needs, or what is now familiarly called "capturing the voice of the customer." The normal method is for a marketing person to probe an opportunity for a new product or new product feature and to feed that information back. The procedure can also be characterized as a translation of what the marketing person hears into his or her language: "The market wants such and such," or "This is what I think the user needs." It is almost a rule of thumb that such comments fail to capture the real need because the original expression of the need has been lost in the translation. No one is communicating. The real need can be transmitted only in the actual voice of the customer. To do this well, members of a product development team must capture the voice of the customer without intermediaries.

At almost all stages of the product development process, ideas need to be communicated between the receivers of information (customers) and the creators of the same information (suppliers). Each can be at any level of an organization: high or low, inside or outside, a maker or a user of a product or service. On Boeing's 777 aircraft project, one of the first team breakthroughs was an agreement establishing ten new levels of design detail and the naming of each level. This gradation, made possible by the sophisticated three-dimensional electronic design tools, allowed a shared language to be developed when discussing deadlines for a "Level III design" or a "Level VI design." Everyone knew the expectations and could thus gauge the effort required. This step in building a common base of communication proved crucial.

> It is the system of management that breeds what goes wrong much more than the inherent complexity of the product systems.

Electronic communication, as fast and efficient as it has become, does not automatically lead to better communication. On the contrary, speed of transmission—real time and all—can mean quicker misunderstanding and faster errors in judgment. For communication to be effective, it must be understood for its content, its subtleties and innuendos, and its intentions. As more and more knowledge sharing within teams is done across cultural and time boundaries, communication becomes more and more difficult.

Exhibit 1-2. Rating your company.

	YES	NO
User needs not grasped		
Finding errors too late		
Management by interference		
Too many projects		
Burnout		
Poor communication		

These six problems that are faced by organizations as they manage the product development process are almost universal. Use Exhibit 1-2 to rate your own company on them. It only takes one no or a weakness of one of the items on the list for things to go wrong. It's Murphy's law.

These all-too-common problems can be tackled and overcome by emulating the experiences of the best do-loopers observed in Japan, North America, and Europe. In Part Two, we discuss specific management practices that can give companies the flexibility, adaptability, and speed necessary to get inside their competition's do loop. These practices do not exist in a vacuum. They are part of a larger perspective that sees a company's actions as interwoven in its structure and sense of mission. In that respect, we have chosen to focus in this book on managing product development as a company-wide strategic processes. It is the first step toward the mastery of the whole.

Notes

1. "Saab Says Car Still Has Bugs," *New York Times*, April 14, 1995.
2. Edith Wilson, "Product Definition Factors for Successful Designs" (thesis, Stanford University, 1990).
3. See Dan Dimancescu, *The Seamless Enterprise: Making Cross-Functional Management Work* (New York: Harper/Business, 1992), p. 31.
4. *BusinessWeek,* September 14, 1992.
5. Ludwig von Bertalanffy, *General System Theory* (New York: Braziller, 1968), p. 48.

Chapter 2
Managing the Whole

The most useful way to understand technology and people within a system is to understand their relationship to the larger whole they serve.

—Marvin Weisbord, *Productive Workplaces*

Companies that try to improve their performance by working on the pieces of the process miss the point. . . . Yet in company after company management works at fixing the pieces instead of redesigning the processes by which the company's work gets done.

—Michael Hammer and James Champy
Reengineering the Corporation

IBM's successful introduction of the Thinkpad in 1993 highlights the difficulty of breaking with a fragmented organizational legacy. To bring this product to market fast, the product manager tossed out the rulebook. "The intent was to break down the functional fiefs in which manufacturing, marketing, and research people were isolated and tended to pursue their own agendas," reported the *New York Times* on June 6, 1993. The same article included a telling anecdote by the project manager, Bruce Claflin:

> By last summer [1992], there was a working model of the first Thinkpad 700C. But there were still institutional problems; the personal computer company may have been reorganized on paper, but old attitudes lingered.

Mr. Claflin recalls a Thinkpad meeting when a colleague objected to some product specifications saying, "I non-concur"—I.B.M.-ese for questioning a decision. Under the old I.B.M. system, a "non-concur" could hold up a decision for months.

Signaling that things had changed, Mr. Claflin replied, "I don't recognize that word." . . . The time for nitpicking had passed. "If we hadn't changed the way we do business, we would have killed the Thinkpad. It would have been smothered by the old management."

The lesson of this anecdote is that a holistic organization is one in which the actions of every part, whether of a department or an individual, are meaningful only in the context of the whole effort. Russell Ackoff of the Wharton School at the University of Pennsylvania puts it this way:

Performance of the whole is not the addition of the performance of the parts, but it is a consequence of the relationship between the performance of the parts. It is how performance relates, not how it occurs independently of the other parts. That is what systems thinking is about.[1]

In other words, it is not enough for an individual to excel in a narrowly prescribed job description or for a single department to do its absolute best within its own boundaries. The individual employee or work unit must constantly recalibrate its actions and decisions to accommodate the larger system's needs. It may mean doing less than the best or, more likely, doing something in a different way. The problem is that most managers are taught, and indeed rewarded, to act independent of the whole. Their boundaries are often narrow and their perspective limited by the department within which they operate. They must be helped to see that the whole and the parts are intermeshed.

In a holistic management system, any one part must continuously adjust its actions to accommodate the needs and requirements of the whole.

Holistic management is an answer to the mushrooming complexity that is overwhelming individuals and organizations in their work. It is the foundation for building agile, flexible organizations by allowing them to respond quickly and effectively to fast-paced change and to ever more complex problems. An array of experiments in various corporations is summarized in Appendix A. Here's how a small study group that gathered in 1993 at Dartmouth College's Thayer School of Engineering (hosted by one of the authors and Dean Charles Hutchinson) described a holistic management system in action:

> One can recognize a holistic system by observing that one part of the system is continuously aware of the interaction of all of its other parts. Holism is also manifested in a system when an external impulse is transmitted to all parts simultaneously, no matter how strong or slight the receipt of the impulse is for any one part. As a result of the impulse, a single part changes its "state" no matter how slightly that might be.
>
> A system can exist within a larger one. This means that a "part" can itself be thought of as a "system" with all its internal characteristics mirrored by the larger whole. A true "holistic system" is organic in that it goes through an aging and maturing process and is always vulnerable to radical change including death.[2]

In any system, change, however small, has a rippling effect over the whole organization, so at any given moment, an entire organization adjusts continuously to changes made somewhere else in the system. "Transitions from one state to another are a characteristic of holistic systems," the Dartmouth group observes. "Those transitions can be of short or very long durations, meaning months to years. During the transition the system is in a state of disequilibrium." This is why an agile and flexible world-class enterprise can be thought of as being in a state of continuous disequilibrium. It is always adjusting to change it perceives in market needs, technology opportunities, new employee competencies, competitive threats, or new regulations.

An agile and flexible world-class enterprise can be thought of as being in a state of continuous disequilibrium.

Following up the Dartmouth meeting a year later at the Abbaye de Villeneuve in Nantes, France,[3] New York University professor Patrick Hoy, a noted essayist and a retired army colonel who also taught at West Point and Harvard, illustrated continuous disequilibrium by drawing a set of dots on one side of a board, each one representing a soldier standing in formation 10 deep and 10 wide. On the other side, he drew a formation with the same number of dots, but 5 wide and 20 deep. "If I order a group to break from one formation and reassemble in the next," he explained, "I need only give the order. I don't tell them how to get there. They just do it. But what's most relevant is that a snapshot of the transition from one formation to the other appears absolutely chaotic and seemingly leaderless."

Hoy's snapshot makes most people uncomfortable because it smacks of disorder and uncertainty. Managers in most companies view moments of disequilibrium as anathema. Rather than seeing it as a necessary and positive adjustment to change, they will try to beat it back and return the organization to its original state. But for an organization to function at its best, to adapt quickly and efficiently to change, these transitional states are essential. This ability defines the world-class corporation. It becomes part of the culture and the reflexive behavior that lead it to compete successfully.

Holistic business environments are burgeoning. Some have been in the making for several decades, though they have never been called holistic; others are more recent. Some are as vast as Silicon Valley's intricate and ever-changing web of supplier networks linked to larger companies such as Apple, Hewlett-Packard, or Sun Microsystems. Others are built on global information systems: Federal Express's and Levi Strauss's global sourcing and delivery networks, Ford's use of global teleconferencing to link car design teams into a single unified group, Procter & Gamble's redesigned global product supply chains, and Chrysler's new Tech Center with integrated platform teams. All manifest a new managerial understanding of holistic systems, but in varied forms. (To determine how holistic your organization is, see the box on page 23.)

In Europe one of the most dramatic turnarounds came in the auto industry at the British Rover Group. Long considered a has-been in terms of styling and quality, the company resurfaced with best-selling models in the 1990s and a resurgence in the U.S. marketplace. "Before we changed," said Chris Lee, a new-model car director at Rover, "teams were little more than coordinated interrelated functions. And this did not function very well at all." Late in 1990, however, influenced by its partner Honda, the company broke a tradition that had long separated engineering and manufacturing. These were fused, and a new structure of business units based on car families was instituted. The emphasis was on treating the entire development process as a single coordinated effort by a single unified team.

Paradoxically, the answer to increasing workplace complexity is to simplify the system of management. Japanese corporations came to terms with just this paradox as early as the 1950s. To compete in world markets, they knew intuitively, they would have to master a new order of complex technical and organizational problems—not the least of these being the control of their production lines, noted at that time for producing low-quality products. They would have to achieve radical productivity and quality improvements measured in $5\times$ and $10\times$ multiples or more just to catch up—or remain a cheap-labor economy. With this as a driving vision, they set out to reinvent the ways in which more complex consumer and commercial products could be developed and delivered to their customers. In retrospect, we can characterize the Japanese manufacturing (not services) management system that ensued as a breakthrough in simplifying and controlling organizational complexity. It allowed the Japanese to do more and better with less labor, less energy, and fewer materials. The results were nothing short of revolutionary in those industries, such as automobiles or consumer electronics, where they concentrated on becoming agile, flexible competitors.

How Holistic Is My Company?

I here is a simple way you can determine whether your company is holistic.

1. Identify a defect or problem encountered by a customer with one of your products and services. This might be a wrong billing charge, a part that broke in a refrigerator, or an order delivered late.

2. Go to a phone and call your own company's main number (headquarters) and say: "I'd like to register a complaint."

3. There are at least three possible reactions to your call:
   a. "I'll connect you right away to someone who can help." This is a good sign.
   b. "You'll have to call this number." That's a hand-off, forcing you to place another call at your expense and time.
   c. "Sir, I really can't help you. This is headquarters." That's a bad sign.

4. When you get to a person from answers *a* or *b*, describe your complaint (it can take up to five or six numbers in some cases to get to the right person) and wait for the reaction:
   a. "We will correct that immediately and greatly appreciate your calling." A good sign.
   b. "I'll write it down and pass it through channels." Not reassuring.
   c. "Thank you for letting us know." A bad sign.

5. Since this is your company that you are calling, you can now follow what happens next to your complaint knowing that it has been heard and probably recorded in some fashion.
   a. If it is registered in a form that is immediately distributed to all those who need to know and a thank-you note is promptly sent to you by someone, that's an excellent sign.
   b. If it is channeled immediately to a department that can do something about it, that, too, is a good but more limited sign.
   c. If it enters a data base and is never seen again, that's a bad sign.
   d. If it vanished into the woodwork, that's a very bad sign.

6. The ultimate test of the procedure is to see whether your complaint reaches the company's executive council at its quarterly meetings when performance data are reviewed.
   a. If it does, you are doing very well, an excellent sign. Of course, the council has to take such data seriously and react appropriately.
   b. If it doesn't reach the council, it's a very bad sign.

The key to a holistic response is whether the whole system is made aware in an expeditious fashion of a customer problem. If only a few people are aware, the system is not operating as a unified team. If no one finds out, it's bad news gone unseen. The same complaint will come right back at you a short time later. That customer will be the first to move on to another vendor if given the choice.

| Paradoxically, the answer to increasing work-place complexity is to simplify the system of management.

J. Womack and his colleagues, D. Jones and D. Roos, pointed out Japan's productivity successes in a best-selling book, *The Machine That Changed the World*.[4] The data they collected offered a dramatic illustration of "the more and better with less" achievement. A glance at the speed of die changes, for example, shows an efficiency almost 15 times that of the United States and Europe (Exhibit 2-1).

The Japanese model for mastering company-wide organizational complexity originated with the famed and oft-quoted management guru, Peter Drucker, in his writings during the 1950s. He advocated a simple but compelling holistic principle of business success that boiled down to a single overriding concept: *Deliver the whole business in the service of the customer*. Drucker's actual words, first penned in 1954, read as follows:

There is only one valid definition of business purpose: to create a satisfied customer. It is the customer who determines what the business is. Because it is its purpose to create a customer, any business enterprise has two—and only these two—basic functions: marketing and innovation.

Actually marketing is so basic that it is not just enough to have a strong sales force and to entrust marketing to it. Marketing is not only much broader than selling, it is not a

Exhibit 2-1. Productivity comparisons.

| | **Average Number for Each Region** | | |
Category	Japan	United States	Europe
Die change time (minutes)	7.9	114.3	123.7
Lead times for new dies (weeks)	11.1	34.5	40.0
Machines per worker	7.4	2.5	2.7
Part defects per car	0.24	0.33	0.62
Number of suppliers per plant	170	509	442

specialized activity at all. It is the whole business seen from the point of view of its final result, that is, from the customer's point of view.[5]

Toyota's leaders recount reading these words during the late 1950s and taking them to heart. "They made sense to us because we had a system that required a lot of cooperation between us and our suppliers," said an executive. "We knew we had to be the best to compete and that cooperation across departments was the key." So they pushed for an organizational style that simplified communication among all parts of the company: the company and its customers, its suppliers, its bankers, and its distributors. To do this they tapped and amplified a base of highly disciplined quality control methods and techniques espoused by such gurus as W. Edwards Deming, Armand Feigenbaum, Kaora Ishikawa, and Joseph Juran: the fundamentals of statistical process control, Deming's check-plan-do-check-act cycle, quality circles, and structured problem solving.

A New System of Management

In the early 1960s, without a clear model or a textbook to guide them, innovative Japanese business leaders set out to create a new system of management. They started by deliberately abandoning the formal structure. "In February 1963, [at Toyota] the existing system of vertical departmental assignment was abolished," wrote Kenji Kurogane, a Japanese expert on cross-function management.

> Under the traditional departmental management system, executives tended to represent their own departmental interests, and consequently interdepartmental cooperation was not realized. To solve this problem, company-wide system reorganization was put into effect. In this new system, executives, although retaining their day-to-day responsibilities, were assigned to multiple cross-functional areas in such a way as to promote the analysis of activities from a company-wide point of view.[6]

In effect, they invented a whole new category of horizontal functions and layered them across the traditional vertical chimneys (Exhibit 2-2). Senior people with specialized vertical competencies took on the added responsibility of working on horizontal teams to address issues requiring company-wide coordination. Lowering warranty costs is an example. A permanent company-wide team would craft a process that everyone could agree to in order to reduce warranty costs consistently over time. This structure was developed in the early 1960s in Japan; it took almost 30 years for the same idea to take root in American firms. By the early 1990s, we renamed these same horizontal functions "strategic processes" and experimented in managing them with cross-organization teams. Such processes as product development, order fulfillment, and quality (warranty cost reduction) became immediate candidates for horizontal management at companies such as Hewlett-Packard, Procter & Gamble, and Milliken.

A Three-Tier Enabling Hierarchy

What evolved from Japan's 30-year experiment of building a new holistic system of management and the Westernization of

Exhibit 2-2. Horizontal process structure.

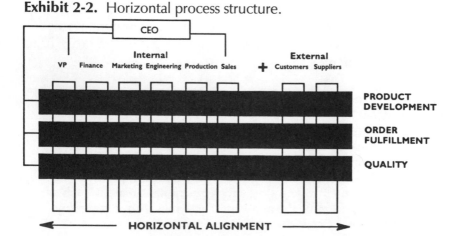

those ideas in the early 1990s is a three-tier concept of management, each tier enabling the effectiveness of the next. (The
phrase *enabling hierarchy* comes from Patrick Hoy. See Appendix
B.) Rather then eliminate hierarchy, this new concept redefines
it. Senior cross-organization teams at the top set goals and determine strategies and objectives for achieving them; midlevel
teams craft and monitor company-wide strategic processes and
build the inventory process methods and tools necessary to meet
the objectives; and lower-level delivery teams, also cross-organi-
zational, execute the day-to-day work. This form of lateral teaming hierarchy is a cornerstone to the style of management from
which our best practices are drawn. This hierarchy, in our view,
constitutes a systemic breakthrough to the management of complex, large, and geographically dispersed organizations.

A lateral teaming hierarchy is a cornerstone to the
style of management from which our best practices are drawn.

At Toyota, and indeed in most other large Japanese companies, these horizontal functions (or *strategic processes,* as we now
call them) focus on two types of company-wide issues: meeting
customer needs and internal support processes. A study of 78
Japanese Deming Prize–winning companies provided the following breakdown of horizontal processes prevalent in them:

Strategic Processes	*Number of Companies*
External customer focused	
Quality/warranty	59
Cost	54
Quantity/delivery	39
New product development	22
Sales/ordering	14
Internal support focused	
Personnel/training	11
Safety	7
Purchasing	6
Information	3

Laterally coordinated strategic processes have a clear purpose: to concentrate on system organization without the burdens imposed by old departmental responsibilities.[7] In this manner, senior line managers interacting *as a cross-organization team* are held accountable for the design and quality of the strategic process and for its improvement. As a consequence, senior executive behavior and the allocation of power—and thus the structure of the organization—must be shifted to a process-driven mind-set. This is no easy task. Ford started to make the shift in 1980 when it constituted Team Taurus as a single company-wide team and out of it launched a new family of cars in 1986. But that company's executives will quickly admit off the record 15 years later that they still had a long way to go in effecting a permanent change in behavior.

Old Ways Die Hard

When GM ran a full-page advertisement in a national business magazine late in 1992 for one of its car models, the backdrop to the car was a traditional pyramid organization chart, presumably intended to connote executive power and influence. By inference, the car pictured in the ad would appeal to people with important titles like those on the organization chart. A few weeks later Chrysler ran a costly three-page pull-out ad that spoofed GM's by running the following banner headline over a similar pyramid chart: "Unfortunately most cars are ruined when they run into barriers like this." The point was made: The old organization chart gets in the way. It depicts a sum of parts. "Teams design cars," touted Chrysler's advertisement.

The effects of compartmentalization are clear from the following story, reported by the *New York Times* on December 29, 1992:

> A survey by the *New York Times* of new car models in 1992 revealed that GM had 61 models with two keys, one for the door and another for the ignition. All Japanese models and most Ford and Chrysler cars had one key for both functions. Why the difference? GM's car doors were produced at one

plant. The steering wheels with ignitions at another. A company engineer acknowledged on the condition of protecting his anonymity that it was an organizational "nightmare" to think of coordinating doors and steering wheels.

In an environment such as the one depicted in GM's own ad, workers' narrowly prescribed tasks are disconnected from the enterprise's customer. Workers can do their utter best, which they often do, and still fail because they are not directly linked to other critical parts of the process. In such an environment, managers can always find someone else to charge with "screwing up." Eventually the person at the top bangs the table, blames others for being dumb, puts out the fire, and gets rewarded. Such behavior has long characterized managers in traditional command-and-control companies. This is *not* what we mean by world-class performance.

The thick cocoon of reward and compensation also makes old habits linger. Over decades these have ossified careers into narrow tracks bounded by a departmental label such as marketing, finance, or engineering. Because managers' promotions and bonuses are based on the number of people who report to them, they create reporting fiefdoms and bloat head counts—the antithesis of holistic management. Organizations whose internal parts are more likely to protect turf than to collaborate will find it difficult to adopt a working principle as basic as Drucker's "delivering the whole business to the customer."

Crafting a New Understanding

The changeover from traditional top-down management structure to a more holistic structure is a shoal-ridden journey, as the experiences of companies such as GM, Ford, and IBM illustrate. It requires a radical shift in perspective and a willingness to give up old habits of control and ingrained reward systems. Just such a change faced an 1,100-employee subsidiary of an American company in Mexico City. Its U.S. corporate headquarters executives were pushing for a flatter organization and significant cost improvements in day-to-day production efficiency.

The Mexican operation's 14-person executive team and one of us brainstormed what was meant by horizontal management, a term cascading down from higher levels in the company. More important, what would it mean in practice? Out of the brainstorming session emerged a listing of 11 processes as candidates for horizontal teaming. These were then prioritized by asking, "What process(es) are absolutely critical to the success of the plant?" The answers made it evident that some of the 11 were not as critical as others and thus fit much better as subsets of other processes. For example, materials processing was seen as a subset of order fulfillment. If orders were late, or in the wrong quantity, or poorly packaged, the client would react and sales would suffer. No one questioned the criticality.

In this manner, a clearer picture of the whole company's processes and their interrelationships came to the light. Some addressed tasks that an individual with a specialized skill could perform, such as taking an order or issuing an invoice. Others, such as running a packing line, involved a combination of specialized tasks and required a small team. Those, in turn, could be aggregated into a top-level process critical to the plant's overall success, such as order fulfillment.

Eventually, the original list of 11 processes was reordered by the management team into a three-tier teaming structure: The top level addressed strategic issues affecting the plant; the middle focused on strategic processes essential to the success of the plant; and at the third, teams took responsibility for executing tasks within each process. In turn, functional departments such as engineering or safety were redesigned as "competence centers," providing skills or specialized support to any of the three levels. Thus evolved a more horizontally integrated structure for managing the whole plant.

Stan Gage, program manager for business process management at Hewlett-Packard in Palo Alto, California, is a corporate pioneer in crafting a new understanding of process-focused management. He describes the kind of dramatic restructuring illustrated in the Mexican plant in the following way: "Adopting a process view of an organization represents a revolutionary change in perspective. . . . A hierarchical structure will depict the organizational responsibilities and reporting relationships whereas a process structure depicts a dynamic view of how the organization delivers value."

> Adopting a process view of an organization repre-sents a revolutionary change in perspective. A hi-erarchical structure depicts the organizational responsibilities and reporting relationships; a process structure depicts a dynamic view of how the organization delivers value.

Gage developed a process hierarchy at Hewlett-Packard that has eight levels:

Level Eight **Company-wide**
Processes that affect all elements of an organiza-tion (e.g., corporate strategic planning; company-wide personnel procedures)

Level Seven **Multiple businesses unit**
Processes shared by logical groupings of more than one business unit (e.g., processes used in common by all divisions making computer pe-ripherals)

Level Six **Single business unit**
First level where key cross-departmental pro-cesses report (e.g., methods for managing a set of processes that characterize a division)

Level Five **Portfolio process**
Methods for managing multiple iterations of any process over time (e.g., product generation pro-cess, order fulfillment process)

Level Four **Single process cycle**
A single iteration of a process from input through output (e.g., product life cycle, shipping a single order)

Level Three **Activity**
A related group of tasks within a process to pro-duce a result (e.g., circuit design, software test)

Level Two   **Task**
                  The basic unit of work performed by individuals
                  (e.g., design capture, module functional test, as-
                  sembly process)

Level One   **Method**
                  The basic technique used by individuals to per-
                  form work (e.g., analytical technique, automated
                  testing)

Looking at process management in this manner, it is easy
to see how the old structure at the Mexico City plant bore no
relationship to the actual processes that needed to be managed.
It was based on who reported to whom. Single supervisors simply oversaw the individual work of a number of employees, each
performing narrowly prescribed tasks. If anything went wrong,
the supervisor was the only person who knew how the process
worked. If the supervisor was sick or transferred, no one else
could fill in. Worse, company policy caused strain and disconti-
nuity by assigning new supervisors fresh out of graduate school
without any prior training. "Crisis management" is what one
manager labeled it. "Every day there are problems that only a
supervisor can handle. If he's not available, everything stops."

With the management group's visualizing its whole operation as an integrated group of plantwide processes, a new picture fell into place. Rather than holding a single overworked
supervisor accountable for a group of workers, each performing
tasks independently, a whole team would be held accountable
for the whole process assigned to it. If anyone was absent, the
others could fill in since everyone understood how their jobs
supported one another.

Another insight was gained from this analysis. Functions—
the kind with a department name and title on the door such as
"engineering" or "warehousing"—lost their old meaning when
the company was conceived as a group of interrelated processes.
The old functional bosses managed budgets and people; for
things to happen functional managers had to come together and
agree. Often, however, they quibbled over turf and argued about
who controlled what resources. When a critical process such as

order delivery was seen as the organizational focus, the functional titles lost their old relevance. The new role of the function was to serve as a competence, offering skills or specialized knowledge to an order delivery process team. Support with the right resources replaced control over resources.

By treating process as the organizational focus, the existing pyramid-style chart was abandoned in favor of a radically different one. The new one showed a large box containing two smaller boxes (Exhibit 2-3). One was labeled "delivery process," meaning the plant operations that manufacture products and fill orders. Within it were several smaller boxes indicating subprocesses managed by teams. The other large box was labeled "product development process," and within it were several subprocesses of the core project team.

Surrounding each of the two dominant processes were symbols representing competencies such as engineering, training and personnel, and safety. And finally, above the new organization chart was drawn a box depicting a Tier 1 senior management team consisting of representatives of each of the main processes and competencies. Its responsibility was to craft the strategy and objectives of the processes that the Tier 2 teams were accountable for deploying. In this fashion, the Mexican plant's management team erased a form of hierarchy based on

Exhibit 2-3. A new teaming organization chart.

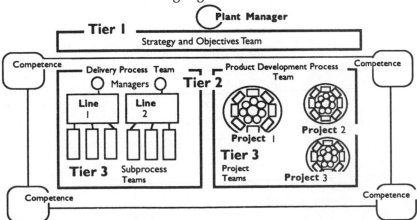

compartmentalized functions in favor of another, far more organic and systemic, that reflected actual beginning-to-end work processes.

A similar structure was developed by Black & Decker, in this case to make product development more effective. "We started in the early 1990s with a very traditional functional development organization," reported Will Hill, a vice president with responsibility for redesigning the organizational structure surrounding product development. "It had all the expected departmental names at the top: mechanical design, electrical engineering, model shop, and so forth." These departments assigned people to participate in product development projects under categories such as saws, cordless, or woodworking. This was the old matrix, two-boss system. The real boss, however, was the one with the resources, the functional department head. The project team did not actually hold control. To break this hold, a new structure, unified operations within a teaming organization, made project delivery teams answerable to a global business unit team (Exhibit 2-4).

The new project teams own the development resources in each of four product categories. They are supported, in turn, by competencies in three strategically important areas: (1) core technologies such as batteries or motors, (2) technical competencies, and (3) other functions, including marketing, manufactur-

Exhibit 2-4. Black & Decker's old and new organizational structures.

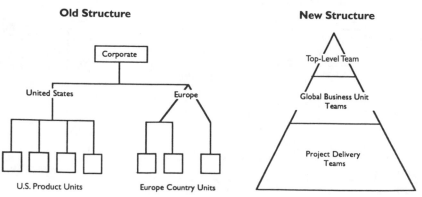

ing, finance, and purchasing. "This system," stated Hill, "empowers the leaders of teams. We have imposed a lot more structure when it comes to setting objectives and in learning how to control the process. The real difference here is that we have gotten away from the single (functional) boss saying 'do this.'"

The teaming focus instituted at Black & Decker and the Mexican operations is implicitly horizontal in that it bridges departmental boundaries. The same intent is visible in other corporations. At Sabre Development Systems (American Airlines), a systems integration software company with 5,000 employees, the old pyramid was abandoned, as were vice president titles. The centerpiece to the new structure are *engagement teams*, each aimed at solving a software systems integration need brought to it by a client—in this case, airports with complex logistical issues such as fuel management, crew assignments, and food. The rest of the Sabre company was redesigned to enable the success of these teams by providing support from centers of excellence—skills in critical technologies such as software languages—or simply by providing infrastructure support through normal human resources, legal, or other services. Each center is responsible for nurturing a critical competence and contracting those competencies to engagement teams. Hierarchy was thus redefined in terms of value delivered rather than simple functional titles (Exhibit 2-5). In this structure the engagement team is the core of the organization.

The redesign achieved a consolidation of system integration solutions into the hands of a single team accountable for the whole process. This eliminated a proliferation of ad hoc teams offering partial, and often incompatible, solutions to a large community of clients. Looking at the same issue from another perspective, Procter & Gamble executive David P. Hanna concluded that "the most common fallacy individuals are guilty of is treating a living, organic system (an organization) as if it were a lifeless piece of machinery. . . . Most managers are appalled by the rigidity and dogma of Machine Theory when they see its principles listed. Yet they manage by these principles every day!" And, he adds, "Too often the piece is not considered in the context of the whole. Irregularities in the system are treated

Exhibit 2-5. Sabre's new organization chart.

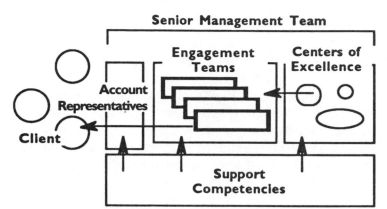

Source: Simplified from presentation by Jim Franke, Managing Director, Sabre Development Systems, to the IAPD, November 1993.

as though they were errors in performance when in some cases they might be caused by changes in the environment."

The value of company-wide process teams is expressed by Marvin L. Patterson, who, as director of engineering at Hewlett-Packard, argued strongly that "the collective expertise on this [process] council represents an essential competitive asset for the company." Referring to the software technology council that met quarterly to discuss software development problems and practices, he added, "Project teams at HP routinely conduct an analysis of completed projects to identify opportunities for improvement. This information is used to advance processes used in subsequent projects. Sharing of best practices that result occurs through a project management council, which also meets quarterly, and through an annual company-wide project management conference."[8] Such events play a vital role in bringing individuals together to share and deliberate on issues with a systemic perspective.

A world-class company remains steadfast in its commitment to deliver the whole enterprise's capabilities to the customer. This is the systemic context in which we see the role of the new management structure such as HP's and the enabling role each level of process hierarchy plays. Built around company-wide strategic processes, the new enterprise is thus better able to harness continuous change to competitive advantage. This ability is central to the mastery of the product development process.

Notes

1. Russell L. Ackoff, "The Second Industrial Revolution" (manuscript, Wharton School of Finance and Commerce, University of Pennsylvania, n.d.), p. 11.

2. Meeting at the Thayer School of Engineering, March 1993, Hanover, N.H. Companies present: American Airlines-Sabre Development Systems, Digital, Hewlett-Packard, Levi Strauss, Procter & Gamble, and several academics in philosophy, computer science, and environmental studies.

3. Meeting hosted by the Institut de l'Homme et la Technologie (IHT), Nantes, France.

4. J. Womack, D. Jones, and D. Roos, *The Machine That Changed the World* (New York: Rawson Associates, 1990).

5. Peter Drucker, *Management* (New York: Harper & Row, 1973), p. 61.

6. Kenji Kurogane, ed., *Cross-Functional Management: Principles and Practical Applications* (Tokyo: Asian Productivity Organization, 1993), pp. 18–19.

7. Jay Galbraith was an early proponent of the horizontal model. See his *Competing With Flexible Lateral Organizations* (Reading, Mass.: Addison-Wesley, 1994).

8. Marvin L. Patterson with Sam Lightman, *Accelerating Innovation: Improving the Process of Product Development* (New York: Van Nostrand Reinhold, 1993), p. 19.

Chapter 3

The Product Development Process

GM has stumbled because its system for developing new models is slow and cumbersome. . . . Design and engineering staffs deteriorated into feudal bureaucracies. . . . They have not been turning the millions of bits of information about what customers prefer into the features and performance characteristics that attract buyers.

—*New York Times*, March 7, 1993

Product lives are now shorter while quantities are higher. We cannot afford to let our customers take months to become aware of our products. Our goal is an electronic web that is pretty much in your face.

—Gian Carlo Bisone, Vice President for Marketing in North America, Compaq, *Fortune*, December 12, 1994

By any measure, product development is more complex than ever. Not only are products themselves more complicated, but the means of selling them, the service necessary to sustain them, and in many cases their environmental impacts are all substantially more complex. This is why managing the process holistically has assumed such importance. It is no longer good enough to manage parts of the process; it is how one manages the whole that differentiates world-class winners from losers.

A starting point for thinking about the whole process is the continuous learning associated with world-class performers. The best *replicate* past successes. They *document* what they do so that they can build on past experience. They *measure* performance in order to gauge progress. And they brainstorm *improvement* actions (Exhibit 3-1). Each of these steps is repeated in an ever-improving spiral. Those that master it achieve exceptional results. As pressures mount on companies to develop better products, faster, and cheaper, disciplined execution of this improvement spiral is a precondition for staying in the game. A graphic depiction of the product development spiral is analogous to the plan-do-check-act spiral developed by quality guru W. Edwards Deming. Information drawn from one cycle fuels the improvement and direction in the next. An ability to sustain the spiral distinguishes world-class practitioners. Achieving it brings one up the five-level process maturity ladder developed by the Software Engineering Institute:

Level Five **Optimizing**
              Process tuning and correcting current unsuitabilities

Level Four **Managed process**
              Quantitative data are collected and used to improve the process

Exhibit 3-1. The continuous learning process.

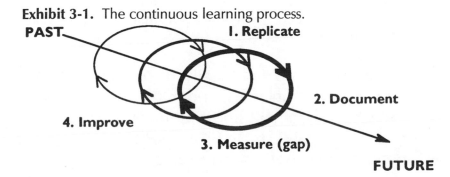

Level Three   Defined process
Framework for process management is established. Only quantitative evaluations of work can be made.

Level Two   Repeatable process
Efficient development of similar problems that have already been developed. Problems with new technologies introduction.

Level One   Initial process
Chaotic process. Difficulties with making and achieving commitments. Frequent changes of plans and procedures. Dependency on exceptional personnel.

Mastery of this spiraling evolution requires deeply rooted changes in managerial behavior, which are often strenuously resisted. One reason is that teams, not individuals, are becoming the principal actors in managing the spiraling loop; another is that senior managers are no longer old-styled "I know best" order givers but champions or mentors of teams. Indeed, management from the top, or what we have called *management interference,* is one of the major problems facing companies wishing to become flexible and competitive. A consequence of these changes is that functions are losing budgetary and staff control while taking on new responsibilities as nurturers of critical competencies. Another consequence, far more profound, is the emergence of a new business culture in which company-wide process management—or the way a beginning-to-end process is accomplished—is taking precedence over narrowly prescribed functional titles.

Treating processes holistically means that much more is being included under the umbrella of product development and that many more players are being asked to share ownership on development teams, from start to finish.

Treating processes holistically means that much more is being included under the umbrella of product development and that many more players are being asked to share ownership on development teams, from start to finish. This is why it is hard, if not impossible, to assign control of so complex a process to a single individual or department. As accountability is redefined, teams are taking on three new areas of responsibility: a widening *span of activity* falling between the start and end dates of a product development cycle, more *control over decisions* in the development process, and the *streamlining of communication* to eliminate unnecessary intermediaries and make the exchange of information more open. These facets are critical to the transfer of accountability from functions into the hands of teams with beginning-to-end control over processes such as product development.

There are several different types of product development projects. We are concerned in this book principally with break-through products, iterative products, and derivatives, and less with a fourth kind, customized products, which are generally one of a kind in character, such as a new class of engines for a fighter jet or software controls for missile systems, and are therefore less replicable.

The first, the most costly, and the most difficult development type of projects is aimed at achieving *breakthroughs* that will leapfrog the competition, sometimes even making headlines. Breakthroughs often lead to a platform change—a basic redefinition of a family of products from the ground up. Many of these bank the house on whether they succeed, as was the case with the Taurus model at Ford in the 1980s or the Alpha chip at Digital in the 1990s. A more recent example is the PowerPC developed by Apple, IBM, and Motorola and intended as a new chip platform for a family of computers. In each case, a chain of products is designed around the platform. A company's platform breakthrough may simply be an incremental component for a more complex system sold by another company. For example, a new wheel braking system platform might be designed to fit into an existing automobile or truck model.

Most product development efforts fall into a second category, called *incremental*. The goal is to build new features into an existing product platform or to reduce manufacturing costs of products already in production—for example, a laptop computer with a brighter screen or a telephone exchange system with an add-on feature of some sort, such as voice mail or automatic forwarding service. Though the less glamorous side of product development, incremental development is relentless in the demands it places on a company's continued innovativeness. Sony and Honda came to dominate the Walkman and motorcycle markets, respectively, by churning out a feverish flow of incremental changes at a pace their competitors were unable to maintain. Compaq fought its way up to number one in PC sales with the same relentless focus on continued incremental changes.

A third type of product is the *derivative*, a category of products sold as an add-on to something already in the marketplace—for example, a computer peripheral such as a printer or a specialized software application. Large numbers of entrepreneurial developers of derivative products, many of them small companies, ride in the slipstream of larger producers of commodity products such as a PC or a car.

Finally there is the world of *customized* products: either one-of-a-kind products, made to the unique requirements of a single customer, or existing products with tailored features added on. Production volumes are often in low quantities. The Department of Defense buys highly specialized military products designed for a unique purpose, such as a fighter aircraft with a narrowly prescribed mission, a radiation-proof satellite, or battle-hardened PCs. The development team typically is driven to meet stringent fixed costs and strict deadline commitments and worries little about sales and merchandising of the product.

For each type of product, a development team's tool kit of management methods and techniques will vary. However chosen, they must accommodate a widening span of beginning-to-end activities, greater decision-making control, and seamless communication essential for a team to be effective.

The Widening Span of Team Accountability

When we founded the International Association for Product Development (IAPD) in 1990, we viewed product development somewhat naively as starting arbitrarily on the day a management go-ahead was given to proceed by authorizing a project budget and a schedule and concluding on the first day of production. But it soon became evident that world-class companies had a much broader conception of the span of activities encompassed in a product development cycle.

Many companies managed this cycle with a fairly standard staging process but carried it beyond initial production to the actual retirement of the product. At Digital, for example, the phase review process started at Phase Zero (Strategy and Requirements) and went all the way through Phase Five (Product Retirement), each phase accompanied by a set of exit criteria. Described in a thick book, the process was to be applied uniformly across all projects. "The Phase Review Process shall be used whenever a specific product is being contemplated," the manual stated. "It is NOT intended to explain HOW a specific group or organization meets these requirements."

Within Digital it was widely and informally acknowledged that considerable effort and investment in actual product development occurred invisibly before Phase Zero. The boundary was in fact quite fuzzy. The most enterprising managers could get a lot of preliminary work accomplished before the formal go-ahead. Because no one knew that considerable work had already been done, the running start made then would look good when it came to meeting subsequent deadlines. What was invisible was the substantial cost in time, money, and effort that went into off-line start-ups, a cost buried somewhere in the accounting system. In fat times, this did not matter. But when things got lean, the inefficiencies of the process were glaring. Off-line use of staff and equipment took resources away from formally authorized projects, and invariably considerable infighting occurred over resource allocations.

By not recognizing and managing the earliest stages of product development, Digital faced another problem: not defining and understanding customer needs. As detailed and seemingly thorough as the phase review process was, Digital was failing to respond to fundamental changes in customer needs. It missed the PC market. It failed to leverage opportunities such as its own pioneering Notes groupware that eventually migrated with its developer to Lotus—and market success. Its product development process, as replicable and as well documented as it was, wasn't being improved in ways that brought the company closer to its customers, current and future ones. Only part of the spiral was being managed.

A novel and broad perspective of the product development came from the Department of Defense (DOD). In 1988, the DOD commissioned a well-crafted and insightful study that came up with its own definition for weapons development and coined the term *concurrent engineering*. Embracing all the activities involved in developing a product from inception to disposal, the term focused attention not only on the initial planning stages of weapons development but also on the obsolescence and actual disposal of weapons systems. This concept introduced downstream environmental issues into the equation by suggesting that they be accounted for in the initial product conceptualization phase—and not ex post facto, as was the norm.

Here's what the study said:

> Concurrent engineering is a systematic approach to the integrated, concurrent design of products and their related processes, including manufacture and support. This approach is intended to cause the developers, from the outset, to consider all elements of the product life cycle from conception through disposal, including quality, cost, schedule, and user requirements. In the sequential method, information flows are bidirectional and decisions are based on consideration of downstream as well as upstream inputs.[1]

Such notions argue for a sharp conceptual break with long-held management practices. Although old-style hand-offs—"It's your problem now"—were no longer acceptable, the authors of the 1988 report emphasized that few companies had found a "best way" of achieving concurrency in their development projects. Within a few short years, that would change.

Hewlett-Packard (HP) developed its own definition of a full product development span. A cycle began, HP developers agreed, not when management gave a go-ahead but when a market opportunity first arose—perhaps on the announcement of a technological innovation or the expression of a need by a customer—and it ended years later with the product's obsolescence. This definition allowed HP to attach an opportunity cost to the time lost between the day the opportunity first arose and when a project actually started, weeks, months, or in some cases years before an effort was actually initiated. The effect was to put a very different twist on the calculation of break-even time: the point at which contributed funds from each sale are large enough to equal the capital and overhead invested in launching the project. It put urgency, too, into a team's frame of reference, allowing the team to look forward to possible changes in the break-even point that might come from unanticipated competitive entries, price changes, and cost overruns and delays.

> By extending the outer boundaries of the product development cycle, the beginning-to-end responsibilities have been made substantially more complex.

By extending the outer boundaries of the product development cycle, the beginning-to-end responsibilities of a development team have been made substantially more complex. In effect, it became much harder to rationalize the assignment of product development ownership or accountability to a single person or department. Given that so many more players needed to be involved collaboratively throughout the process, they could function only as a unified team with common goals and not as a collage of individually managed project segments.

This is illustrated in the coordination of the "fuzzy front end" when the overall project criteria are determined. It means forging direct links to those who formulate strategy, to potential and actual customers, as well as to marketing people, technologists, or regulatory specialists who might otherwise be content working at arm's length. In other words, the broader the span of activity encompassed by product development is, the greater is the interaction required between developers, suppliers, and customers. Because mastery of this early coordination is still widely acknowledged as a Western Achilles heel, it still offers an opportunity for high-leverage $10\times$-type improvements of the sort emphasized in the best-practice chapters that follow in Part Two.

In a similar fashion, at the downstream or "fuzzy after launch" end of product development, there is growing awareness of the importance of distribution, promotion, logistics, service, and disposal impacts far earlier in the product development process. This includes environmental issues that may arise out of stricter regulatory requirements or safety and liability issues associated with products and services.

> A new awareness of the broad systemic span of product development is the real novelty of the 1990s.

This new awareness of the broad systemic span of product development is the real novelty of the 1990s. It results in development teams' treating the creation of new products as part of a wider and more comprehensive web of interactions. And given the rapid evolution toward extended enterprises, teams soon expand to include external partner firms, suppliers, and customers. Some firms, such as Procter & Gamble, even treat regulatory agencies to which they "supply" approval documentation as "customers." By formatting documentation to the government's specifications, the federal regulatory cycle can be shortened by many months—even years. This was one of Boeing's payoffs in the 777 aircraft development process. By incorporating the Federal Aviation Administration's regulatory needs into the front-end design, Boeing was allowed to skip a two-year test phase and thus could enter the market two years earlier.

In addition, electronic information technologies have evolved so rapidly that real-time information exchange is now a given. Not only is there less control from a central source, but ideas, features, and materials are tested in real time. The consequence is little or no time for delays caused by moving memos around or circulating information on paper in order to solicit reviews and decisions. One benefit of real-time communication is that developers, suppliers, and customers can discourse on preferred options before a cent of production money is spent. In such a setting, old-style management layers are an impedance to quick action.

Control Over Decisions

Any product development activity follows a set of sequential steps. Each contains a logical grouping of value-adding activities carried out collaboratively by various parts of an organization and its suppliers. Steps (or phases, as most companies term them) are generally gated by a formal decision point. These decisions might require redoing work or, in an extreme case, might lead to halting the project itself if basic requirements cannot be met. They serve as well to establish precise points at which corporate funding commitments, often very large and irreversible, are confirmed. Thus, the discipline imposed by key gating decision points becomes a critical success factor in the development of new products.

The discipline imposed on key gating decision points is one of the critical success factors in the development of new products.

The examples in Exhibit 3-2 show the logical flow these steps take and suggest the differences in how companies characterize the beginning and ending points of the product development process. Strict new environmental laws in some countries are forcing the disposal of products such as washing machines and computers to become the responsibility of the producer. Hence, "disposal" is a new step in the product development process for which teams are becoming accountable.

As companies cope with the complexity of issues associated with products they develop, the evolution of the design through to production is treated hierarchically. Toshiba, for example, has a nine-phase procedure for a large and complex integrated software system (Exhibit 3-3). The flow starts with a high-level system planning perspective before being broken down into

Exhibit 3-2. Examples of sequential phases.

A copier company: Five-phase process

Information Collection	Planning	Design	Production and Marketing Preparation	Production and Marketing

A sewing machine company: Seven-phase process

Research and Study	Planning	Design	Fabrication and Prototype	Trial Mass Production	Mass Production	Marketing and Service

A cosmetics company: Five-phase process

Plan	Develop and Design	Trial Production	Mass Production	Sales and Service

subsequent steps that focus more and more narrowly on individual parts. As the process moves closer to conclusion, it builds back up to a review of the whole system being designed and a final confirmation that the initial customer requirements have been met. Only then is the product released to the market.

The same Toshiba process can be taken to another level of detail: Each phase concludes with a review and a decision, indicated by triangular symbols above and below. To carry out reviews in a disciplined fashion, procedures are documented at each phase. These documents are listed under each phase (Exhibit 3-4). Additionally, each phase calls for tests and reviews to establish whether the development process is evolving as planned and whether the product is designed to function as called for by the initial user requirements (Exhibit 3-5). This integrated, or systemic, approach can reduce the impact of errors and cut down substantially on both employee hours and time to accomplish the full cycle. If the process appears complex, it is. So, too, is the software being developed. However, if this approach is managed by a team, the process is greatly simplified by eliminating hand-offs and the risk of passing errors or miscalculations on to the next responsible party. Part of a team's effectiveness comes from the premium it places on communication and information sharing among all members of the team.

Exhibit 3-3. Toshiba's product development process.

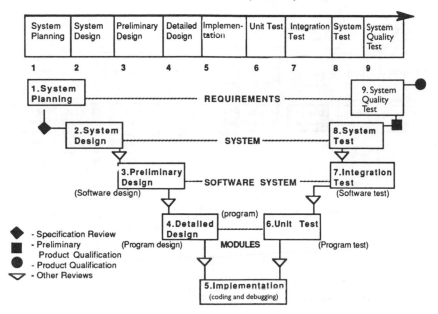

Exhibit 3-4. Toshiba's documenting system.

System Planning	System Design	Preliminary Design	Detailed Design	Implemen-tation	Unit Test	Integration test	System Test	System Quality Test
System (user's) require-ments specifi-cation	Software require-ments specifi-cation	Program require-ments specifi-cation	Module require-ments specifi-cation	Modules	Programs	Software system	System	Quality system
						Software user manual	System opera-tion manual	System mainte-nance manual
	Software develop-ment plan		Unit test specifi-cation		Integra-tion test specifi-cation	System test specifi-cation		
	Software quality plan				Unit test report	Integra-tion test report	System test report	Software release notice

Exhibit 3-5. Toshiba's testing and review system.

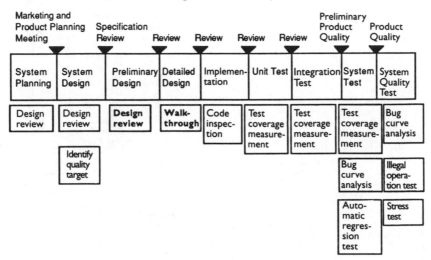

Seamless Communication and Information Sharing

The crucial role that information sharing and communication play in the product development process can be illustrated somewhat eclectically with a long-gone social and cultural institution at MIT, the F&T Diner. Modest in appearance, smelling of burned fat, and often clouded by smoke from its burger broiler, the F&T was *the* place where the famous and not so famous from MIT came to eat, exchange gossip, and put deals together. It was not the good food they came for; it was the opportunity to meet people, catch wind of a new idea, slip in a rumor or two, and exchange concepts on a napkin. Some people say that the technological success of Route 128 was conceived in the F&T Diner in back-of-the-envelope deals between venture capitalists and technologists.

The diner is now gone, though it stood on wooden supports for many years behind a rehabilitated factory five blocks away. Some speculate that the recession that long strangled Greater Boston's high-tech community started when the F&T was dismantled.

The lesson behind this anecdote has to do with information

and how it flows. The F&T was really in the business of managing information, although its owners would have little recognized this part of their business.

Most successful organizations, whether they are companies, universities, or even cities, have an F&T Diner, literally and figuratively. The objective is to optimize a process by *maximizing the opportunity for interaction and information sharing between participants*. The key word is *opportunity*. The goal is to leave the door as wide open as possible for people to engage in unstructured interactions so they can exchange ideas and information openly with serendipitous results.

It is not always that way. Inadequately nurtured communication is an enormous obstacle to fast, flexible product development. Less than a half-mile away from the F&T stand Polaroid's headquarters in a low concrete building in a modern quad surrounded by high-rise buildings housing other parts of the organization. When Sheldon Buckler, vice chairman of the company, spoke to the IAPD on one occasion, he lamented the lack of communication among various parts of the organization: "We forgot how to talk together, how to be innovative." At Polaroid there is no F&T Diner. There is no place to engage in serendipitous information sharing. In contrast, National Semiconductor, one of Silicon Valley's older companies, found itself hampered by having a vast network of unconnected buildings on a single site. To induce people to interact more informally, the company recently constructed a large and inviting eating area surrounded by a well-landscaped park. The effect has been to bring people together at all times of day for casual meetings and on many occasions for more formal company announcements.

A true, world-class enterprise treats information as a dynamic and vibrant resource that travels as much through people and their conversations as it might electronically.

A true, world-class enterprise treats information as a dynamic and vibrant resource that travels as much through people and their conversations as it might electronically. "When a wave of information spreads out broadly everywhere in the organization," states Margaret Wheatley, author of the acclaimed book *Leadership and the New Science,*

> instead of collapsing into just a few interpretations, many moments of meetings—hundreds, even thousands of them—will occur. At each of those intersections between an observer and the data, an interpretation will appear, one that is specific to that act of observation. . . . The multiplicity of interactions can elicit many of those potentials, giving a richness to the data that is lost when we restrict information access to only a few people. An organization swimming in many interpretations can then discuss, combine, and build on them. The outcome of such a process has to be a much more diverse and richer sense of what is going on and needs to be done.[2]

Astra Hässle, a 1,200-person pharmaceutical research laboratory in Gothenburg, Sweden, constructed a new building complex in 1994 with just this in mind. The architectural layout is designed to foster spontaneous contact in corridors, convenient meeting places, and a vast eating area. Oticon, a Danish company, the third largest maker of hearing aids in the world, is another example. As part of a top-to-bottom reorganization, the company "realized that the more radical transformation is from written to verbal communication." Meetings are encouraged throughout the building. Coffee bars are placed in well-traveled open places. "Each coffee bar is the site of about 20 meetings a day averaging ten minutes and 2.7 participants each. . . . Oticon has created an organizational pattern that supports great freedom of action for individuals and teams. They have tied it together with a minimum of hierarchy."[3]

This was a goal, too, at Black & Decker when company leaders restructured around company-wide product businesses. They started with an organization chart organized by country and by product lines within each country. This structure had the debilitating effect of hampering smooth and quick communication across organizational and geographic boundaries and the additional costly effect of causing each country to duplicate product development efforts. A power drill in England was unlike one in Belgium or the United States. When this structure didn't work, it was replaced by a three-tier teaming hierarchy: the corporate team at the top that strategizes and sets objectives, the next tier down consisting of business teams focusing on a product line globally, and then project teams. At each level artificial barriers to information sharing have been removed.

The following example illustrates the same principle from another corporate perspective:

> Goodyear Tire & Rubber has created an information system that allows its 500 salespeople and field engineers to tap into the company's mainframe. Says Al Cohn, marketing manager for commercial systems: "We've got six years' worth of performance data, such as statistics on tread wear, durability, and fuel economy, as well as information on pricing, tire sizes, and competitors' products. When you have that much information you need a mainframe. . . . During a sales call we hook into the mainframe by phone and can answer specific questions from the customer—for example, how a particular tire performs on Mack trucks that haul coal in Kentucky with an average load of 6,000 pounds per tire. In eight or ten seconds we can generate a graph with the answer and print it out. In the old days, people would ask questions like these, and we'd say, 'Sure, let us look in our files, and we'll get back to you in two weeks.' "[4]

When we benchmarked Japanese methods of communication between product development teams and their customers, a multigated process surfaced. All organizational units are encouraged, if not required, to maintain direct contact with customers. This is done to discourage the loss of meanings that would otherwise occur if information traveled up and down formal channels of communication. The goal is to keep the links as short as possible and the purity of the information exchange as high as possible.

These examples and many others confirm the observation of academics such as Professor Edward Lawler of the University of Southern California who concludes that "the horizontal movement of information is what distinguishes a high involvement organization from a control-oriented one."[5]

With accountability transferred to teams, a wider span of activities to manage, decision making far more in their control, and communication freed of artificial constraints, product development takes on a wholly new character.

Notes

1. Robert Winner et al., "The Role of Concurrent Engineering in Weapons Acquisition," Institute for Defense Analyses, Report R-338, 1988.

2. Margaret Wheatley, *Leadership and the New Science* (San Francisco: Berrett-Koehler, 1992), p. 65.

3. Clifford and Elizabeth Pinchot, *The End of Bureaucracy and the Rise of the Intelligent Organization* (San Francisco: Berrett-Koehler, 1993), p. 264.

4. Alison Sprout, "Getting Mileage from a Mainframe," *Fortune,* January 10, 1994.

5. Edward F. Lawler III, *The Ultimate Advantage: Creating the High-Involvement Organization* (San Francisco: Jossey-Bass, 1992), p. 218.

PART TWO

We have all experienced times when, instead of being buffeted by anony-mous forces, we do feel in control of our actions, masters of our own fate.

That is what we mean by optimal experience.

—Mihaly Csikszentmihalyi, *Flow*

Chapter 4
Best Practices

Professional opinion diverges widely on what is really meant by a best practice. But clarifying the meaning is important, particularly if a company is about to risk altering its way of operating by applying someone else's best practice. It better work and there better be evidence of it. But what kind of evidence? At one extreme are those who seek statistical justification. This approach favors sampling a sufficiently large number of cases in order to extract a single best practice and justifying its utility by quantifiable measures of the benefits. In short, if most people are doing it, it must be right. If, for example, more than 50 percent of a sample of companies with high rates of market share use formal technical reviews, is this conclusive evidence that technical reviews are the cause of the success? The only answer is "maybe" because there are so many other variables to consider.

Another approach to identifying best practices, and the one we have favored, is qualitative. As we have seen, a new style of management emerged in the 1990s, its principal characteristic being a holistic approach to managing complex problems. Horizontal processes, a dominant feature of this management style, are a filter through which we tested the merits of a practice. One of the key tests we sought to meet was whether it delivered the whole enterprise to the customer. In short, did the particular practice encourage a holistic solution? Another test was whether the practices offered a robust answer to one or more of the problems we came to see as pervasive. We did not attempt to tackle purely technical problems but focused instead on organizational and management issues relevant to product development.

In 1990, when the IAPD started its best-practice search, the early up-front stages of the product development cycle were viewed as the weakest link in Western practices. Over the two-year period of study, the IAPD not only validated the merit of this focus but also discovered that the early product definition stages are much more complex and extended far sooner than originally believed. By 1995, as more and more companies learned to wrestle with the up-front issues, the importance of dealing with downstream concerns, such as environmental impacts and the accelerated obsolescence of products, became more evident as an emerging best-practice zone. These concepts are illustrated in Exhibit 4-1.

Our process starts by identifying successful companies in selected industries according to profitability, growth of market share, or customer satisfaction ratings. This done, methods and techniques associated with the success are isolated as best practices. When it comes to tackling the problems of user needs, an example of a best practice is the disciplined and replicable product definition process developed over several years by Hewlett-Packard. When it comes to managing error rates, the case of NEC-NIMS (Nippon Electric Corporation's integrated chip design subsidiary) emerges as a world-class exemplar. An exhaustive analysis of the company's procedures prepared by its president, K. Uchimaru, as a step toward winning the acclaimed Deming Prize, highlights a variety of practices, any one of which could be termed best in the world. Based on lengthy meetings and discussions with Uchimaru, we selected his views on reviews and his extensive use of quality function deployment as a problem-solving tool as world-class best practices.

When it comes to avoiding management by interference and empowering teams, Corning Company, headquartered in upstate New York, stands out. Early in the 1990s, it redesigned the company-wide reward and recognition system. Significant plant-level performance improvements, called Goalsharing, are attributed to these innovations. This system gives teams control over aspects of their performance criteria and links compensation to the meeting of the overall performance of the organization. "The result was completely counter recessionary and surprising to all of us," reported a senior executive.

In the case of instituting good communication across organizational boundaries, Toyota and Komatsu stand out as innovators. One technique used is a form of process mapping that integrates four variables onto a single sheet of paper: (1) team

Exhibit 4-1. Product development stages.

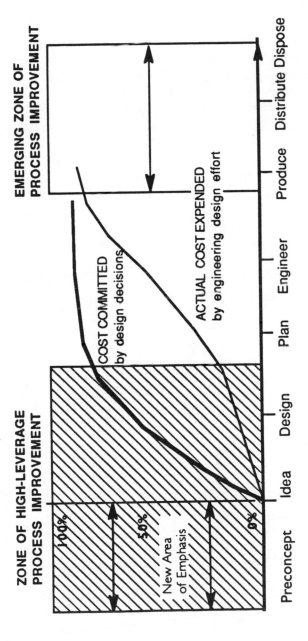

members, (2) stage gates, (3) major events and activities that are executed by one or several team members, and (4) standards or guidelines applying to any single event, activity, or decision depicted on the map. Pioneered in the United States by one of us under the name *"four-fields mapping,"* we present it as a best practice in building effective cross-organization communication and a holistic approach to the management of any complex endeavor. In this manner, we have identified ten categories of best practice, all addressing management-related aspects of product development (Exhibit 4-2).

The best practices, which are detailed in the chapters that follow, will help overcome some of the problem areas we have emphasized. But to some readers, the primary, and perhaps only, value of these practices may be as a benchmark against which to evaluate their own enterprise's capabilities. We detail these practices knowing full well that they are a moving target or a work in progress, evolving with each effort to apply them. They can be read much as one might read a travel guidebook in search of clues and insights into places one will visit.

Exhibit 4-2. Where best practices can help.

The Problem Areas

Best Practices	User Needs Not Understood	Finding Errors Too Late	Management by Interference	Too Many Projects	Burnout	Poor Communication
1. Strategic process teaming			o	o	o	
2. Four-fields mapping			o		o	o
3. Rigorous reviews	o	o	o			o
4. Voice of the customer	o	o				o
5. Metrics		o		o		o
6. Three-track technology management	o		o	o		
7. Suppliers' partners	o	o				o
8. Collaboratory knowledge	o		o	o	o	o
9. Rewards and recognition		o	o	o	o	
10. A new structure			o			o

Chapter 5

Strategic Process Teaming

The processes that integrate the lateral dimensions of organizations are achieving importance equal to that of the hierarchical processes.

—Susan Albers Mohrman, in Jay Galbraith et al.
Organizing for the Future

With a company-wide system in place, effective management is expected . . . by concentrating upon system organization without the burdens imposed by old departmental responsibilities.

—Zenzaburo Katayama, president
Japan Systems Corporation

Teaming is the people side of strategic process management. When it comes to product development, team organization has several dimensions. Professional sports are a useful analogy for the three-tier hierarchy introduced earlier. At the top, a management team strategizes and sets objectives. In the middle, a training and coaching team crafts a process that will select, train, and prepare the players. And on the field, players organize themselves to deliver a winning game by acting as a single unit.

So, too, in the new world of developing products, a team at each tier crafts a process it will follow, fine-tunes it, acts, and then checks what it has accomplished. The Tier 1 team sets the objectives; the Tier 2 process team provides methods, tools, and techniques and monitors the delivery; the Tier 3 project teams adopt and adapt them to the job to be done and carry out the project. In the best cases such teams function as a seamless group of individuals working collaboratively with a systemic perspective of the process. It is not always that way. Activities in many companies are compartmentalized. Individuals act within a narrow boundary of responsibility and leave it to someone else to worry about how to cement all the talent together. This is analogous to putting together an All-Star sports team. Each player may be a superb athlete, but a bunch of superathletes does not necessarily make a winning team. Each tends to show off his or her own talent independent of the others.

Understanding Teaming

Given that teaming is a very old subject and so much has been said and written about it, why is it that so many product development teams are ineffective? Fifty executives, managers, and academics met to talk about this question in July 1993 at a unique meeting at Wake Forest's Graylyn Conference Center in North Carolina, and several smaller groups were organized to attack the question. One of them constructed a fish-bone diagram decomposing problems in product development teaming (Exhibit 5-1). The members agreed that consistent motivation was the biggest problem they faced in their respective companies.

When the issue of "difficult to motivate performance consistently" was discussed in greater depth, the same group found that almost all the critical inhibitors had to do with issues for which senior management was ultimately responsible (Exhibit 5-2): rewards, organizational barriers, team recognition, career implications, or even the call to action. None of the problems had to do with whether individuals were talented.

Step by step, the discussion group at Graylyn reached an important conclusion about the larger U.S. corporate world: No one has teaming right. The problem was systemic, and the group concluded, not unexpectedly, that good teaming starts at

Exhibit 5-1. Problems in product development teaming.

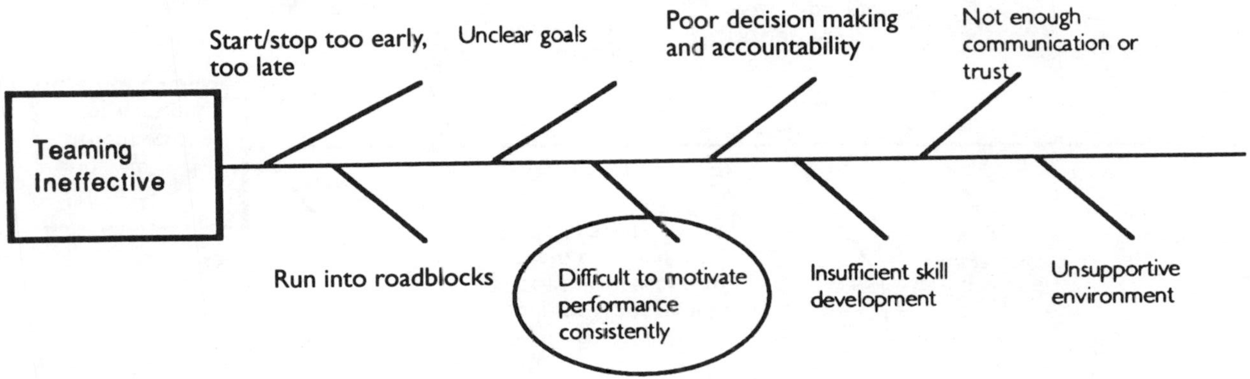

Exhibit 5-2. Critical inhibitors of motivation.

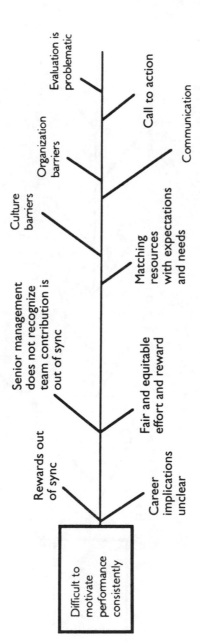

the top. What was new and different about this discussion? In brief, one cannot expect employees on delivery teams, who do the real work on the playing field, to act cohesively if senior managers do not do so themselves and serve as mentors to those below them. One way to put this to the test is to ask the following question of any CEO: "Is product development strategically important to your company's success?" The answer in nine out of ten cases will be yes. Then ask: "Who owns the responsibility for the success of product development?" and the answer will invariably be the name of an *individual:* "Well that's so and so." Usually it is the vice president of engineering, or the vice president of technology; sometimes it is the marketing vice president. It's rarely a company-wide senior team that includes the president or managing director.

"In big companies you rarely see management fully engaged in the early homework that goes into a product development cycle. And," says Professor Steven Wheelwright of Harvard, "they are most likely to be visible when crises happen much later in the process when a project is late, costing too much, or not meeting expectations."[1]

In one organization, a billion-dollar manufacturer of industrial and housing equipment, the CEO delegated responsibility for product development to a vice president of technology. The individual was extremely capable but had no control over product development budgets—functional managers did—and exercised influence only through a team of eight program managers who headed up development teams comprising individuals who reported to their functional leaders. If anything went wrong, if new procedures were required, or if internal coordination needed higher-level influence, the program manager would have to go to the vice president of technology for help. He, in turn, would have to approach his functional vice president peers—those with the operating budgets—to get agreement on a required change. In some cases, the CEO had to be asked to break logjams.

Setting the stage for cross-organization collaboration may be the single most important action that senior management can take to stimulate effective product development. That is what is meant by strategic process management: setting the right goals, eliminating all the barriers, and providing the methods and tools necessary for a delivery team to work at peak efficiency. This role becomes even more critical in an extended enterprise with external partners.

Strategic process management is systemic. It looks at the whole job that must be accomplished and creates whatever senior team is necessary to tackle the whole process. The development of new products and services is treated as a company-wide activity involving all of the traditional functions: marketing, sales, engineering, purchasing, legal, and finance. In a systemic approach it is understood that only by coordinating these functions *at the top first and then down* can one begin to tackle the complexity and risk inherent in most product development programs. If senior management cannot master product development issues as a team, how can anyone lower in the organization?

> If senior management cannot master product development issues as a team, how can anyone lower in the organization?

Once an executive committee has strategized and set goals for an organization, teams of senior line executives or managers can be assigned to oversee each of the strategic processes necessary to achieve the goals. These senior process teams build consensus around common goals in product development, for example, and establish collaborative work practices. More important, their job is to pull down the barriers that may stand in the way of cross-organization relationships.

Do-loop companies maximize opportunities for cross-organization relationships and organize teams around the horizontal process, not the function. Yet surprisingly few Western companies are committed at the top to a consistent and ongoing teaming process that meets these conditions.

In the United States, Hewlett-Packard stands out as one of the exceptions. Jon R. Katzenbach hits the nail on the head when he summarizes HP's approach in a well-crafted and popular book he coauthored, *The Wisdom of Teams*. Reporting on the company's Government Electronics Group (GEG), he writes:

The performance goal was to get both external and internal customers the supplies and materials they needed when they needed them at the lowest possible cost. To do this, GEG's leadership knew it had to move away from an organization emphasizing individual and functional accountability to one that focused on developing teams that began with suppliers and finished with customers.[2]

Our findings suggest that the best do-loopers share important teaming characteristics.

Important Teaming Characteristics

1. A Senior Team of Line Executives Is Accountable to the CEO or Executive Committee for the Design, Objectives, and Monitoring of the Process

In product development, this approach was first manifest at HP in 1989 in two senior process teams. One, the Product Generation Team, focused on hardware products, and the other concentrated on software. Each team pulled together all the functional owners, such as engineering or finance, to agree collectively on a preferred process and the preferred support tools. In this manner, each senior management team designed and owned the responsibility for the quality of the process. Each individual on the team thus gained a shared understanding of the totality of the product development process and set the stage for delivering the whole enterprise's capabilities to the customer. This knowledge was then made available to each of the corporation divisions to use as they saw fit.

A senior management team designed and owned the responsibility for the quality of the process. Each individual on the team thus gained a shared understanding of the totality of the product development process.

In most large Japanese manufacturing companies, strategic process teams are responsible for cross-organization functions such as quality, cost, delivery, production, purchasing, personnel, education, safety, hygiene, information systems, or total quality control promotion. At Toyoda Loom Works, the parent company to Toyota automotive,

> an executive of the main office is assigned as chairman [of a team], and senior managers of the division offices are members. Together, they establish objectives for each cross-function, confirm achievement status, and assume responsibility for consolidation, coordination, support, and information exchange for the division offices.[3]

The same structure is replicated within each division.

The senior process team is held accountable by the CEO for setting the objectives and for the quality of the process as executed by delivery teams who execute the day-to-day work. If objectives are not met in product development, the senior process team is responsible *as a group*—and rewarded or recognized accordingly. If the quality of the process is flawed, the group is responsible for brainstorming and implementing its improvement.

| The CEO delegates permanent ownership of a strategic process and its objectives to a group of senior line people, each of whom brings a "vertical" competence to the table.

The senior titles may vary—vice president, director, or functional head, for example—but the goal is the same: to put into the hands of a senior management team the responsibility for managing a whole beginning-to-end process. Exhibit 5-3 illustrates team membership for two processes.

Given that the process is judged to be strategically important to the success of a company, as is true of product development, it warrants serious time and attention by the line executives responsible for it. The experience of Japanese and

Exhibit 5-3. Process team members.

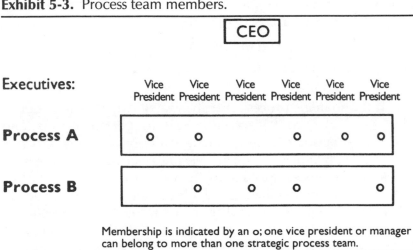

Membership is indicated by an o; one vice president or manager can belong to more than one strategic process team.

Western firms suggests that between 15 and 30 percent of their time is spent not putting out fires but monitoring and mentoring the process. One of the tasks is to set objectives after gathering and analyzing data periodically. They are best monitored quarterly and adjustments made as necessary. Agreements are negotiated on allocating resources controlled by senior line personnel in order to ensure the successful implementation of the process by delivery teams. The requirements for information sharing must be understood and the means and tools for doing so developed. For example, if early market intelligence is a significant component of a product development process, each line officer would agree in advance to contribute critical insights on his or her own area of expertise: regulatory issues, customer needs, supplier capabilities, or new technology trends, for example. In this way, the whole process is treated as a collaborative relationship involving the whole company rather than as a collage of tasks executed in isolation by a function such as marketing.

The senior line team is held accountable, too, for educating employees reporting directly to it in the process design and for propagating the necessary process know-how as widely as possible.

The strategic process and its tool kit of preferred methods and techniques constitute a corporate asset from which a company can exact substantial advantage over less-well-managed competitors.

If the strategic process is truly strategic, the team responsible for it will remain in place for a long period of time, and hence be a permanent component of the organizational structure. In this manner, the CEO delegates permanent ownership of a strategic process and its objectives to a group of senior line people, each of whom brings a distinct competence or responsibility to the table. Their ability to work together constitutes a strategic process capability with a tool kit of preferred methods and techniques from which a company can exact substantial advantage over less-well-managed competitors.

2. Project or Program Core and Extended Delivery Teams Implement the Process and Are Accountable to the Senior Team for the Execution and Results

Delivery teams are the doers; their job is to meet the objectives set for them. But as the complexity of projects increases and outsourcing and strategic alliances become more and more prevalent, the structure of development teams has changed. To bring continuity and coherence to projects, dedicated core team members are engaged full-time from beginning to end.

The core group must be sized appropriately and must represent the right balance of skills and competencies. At Ford Motor, the Taurus Project, a five-year $3.5 billion project, started with a group of about 15 core team members. The Boeing 777 aircraft program, although more complex in scope, had a core design-build team with five principal members representing each of the main subcomponents of the aircraft, headed by two coleaders, themselves high-level executives—one from engineering and one from operations, which assembles the craft. The core group managed a structure of 220 design-build subteams, each with its own core group of five to six main contributors.

At Rover's automotive operations, a new teaming structure

was built around 12- to 15-person teams with complementary skills. "One of the first things we did," said project leader Chris Lee, "was to go out as a group on a fact-finding mission. We spent one month to determine what was expected of us compared to the degrees of freedom and constraints built into the project." From this effort the scale of the business challenge became evident. This led to a three-day off-site meeting during which the team collectively determined its deliverables. A series of follow-up sessions were held to get full closure on the criteria, and a set of key performance indicators and results measures was agreed to. This intense planning effort by the team led to the formulation of a project plan that was approved by management quickly and efficiently. As the project unrolled, it became evident that the homework would pay off; cost, quality, and timing targets were met, and the profit projections on anticipated sales of this model looked "very good" in Lee's words.

There is more to a product development team, however, than just having core members. There is a relationship between the core and its extended part-time members, and a distinction between full-time and part-time participants is important in planning resource allocations and budgets. The extended members fit into two categories: *suppliers* and *customers.* And each of those can be divided into two subcategories: *external* and *internal* to the organization (Exhibit 5-4).

The delivery team structure of core, suppliers, and custom-

Exhibit 5-4. Delivery team organization.

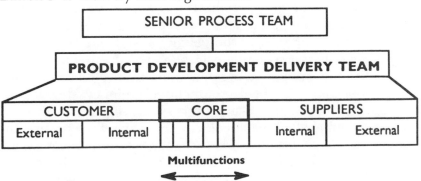

ers was used at Digital to distinguish roles in a variety of successful projects. Suppliers include any specialized resources of
competencies needed by the core team, whether an in-house
skill or a capability contracted from a supplier or a partner firm.
Designating these entities as suppliers creates both an explicit
and implicit understanding that they are delivering a value-adding service to the core team. Therefore, the core team must be
explicit in defining its requirements for those services early and
clearly.

This broader definition of supplier relationship is leading
many firms to replace traditional functions, such as engineering,
with core competencies in precise value-adding technical areas.
Competencies that are not strategically important are contracted
for externally.

> An emphasis on competencies is one of the most
> important breakthroughs in moving away from
> functional chimneys.

Chrysler took this direction when it reconfigured its new and
lavish billion-dollar Tech Center to support five new truck or car
platform development teams, such as the LH series of vehicles,
each located in a large central area of a floor. Each platform team
is supported by office wings containing core competencies, such
as engines or transmissions. These competencies, because they
are deliberately concentrated in a single physical location, constitute a vital critical mass of knowledge. In day-to-day practice
it means that a highly specialized engineer supplies a competence to a platform group in the open platform area and returns
anytime to his or her home competence area in one of the wings.

An emphasis on competencies, as noted in Exhibit 5-5, is
one of the more important organizational innovations in moving
away from compartmentalized functional chimneys as key players on the organization chart. Process teaming diminishes the
power of old-style functional chimneys by transferring the
power to delivery teams that become the "buyers" of competencies. For companies like Chrysler and Boeing, it is a change that
is yielding enormous payoffs. For Chrysler, that payoff is mea-

Exhibit 5-5. Team membership.

PRODUCT DEVELOPMENT DELIVERY TEAM

CUSTOMERS		CORE	SUPPLIERS	
External	Internal		Internal	External
				Competencies		

◄————————— *Extended to include outsiders* —————————►

sured in an engineering design team for the LH and Neon cars of 770 individuals, half the traditional head count, and time to production almost 30 percent shorter. At Boeing, it is manifest in the "snapping together" of its first production airplane and its ability to incorporate client airline companies' needs tightly into the design process.

Another innovation is the relationship of the core team to its "customers." One group at Digital took the unusual step of treating its own management as a customer. "Doing so forced us to solicit management's 'requirements,'" said the team leader, Michael Kleeman. "We then incorporated them into the team's list of customer requirements that had to be met." The term *customer* can include end users, distributors, or even public regulatory agencies. Procter & Gamble (P&G) reluctantly agreed to include distributors as team members late in the 1980s. Wal-Mart, although technically a distributor, demanded that P&G treat it like a customer and do business on its terms. A joint team was established with participants from each company and its own offices at a remote location away from both companies' headquarters. The product improvements they jointly developed in package sizes, delivery methods, and billing were instrumental in tripling Wal-Mart sales of P&G products.

Companies that depend heavily on government agencies for regulatory approval of new products have found that treating government agencies as customers has led to step-changes in performance. In one case, by thinking of the FDA (Food and Drug Administration) as a customer, an organization better understood its requirements for drug or food approval. This understanding allowed information submitted to the agency to be formatted for quicker circulation and analysis and thus lead to quicker product introductions. In the pharmaceutical and bio-technology industries, six months or a year of gained time can mean a difference of hundreds of millions of additional sales revenues and profits and for consumers speedier availability of beneficial drugs.

3. The Charter Spells Out the Project or Program Constraints and Empowers a Team to Act Around Explicit Expectations

When a core team is constituted and a leader designated, one of the empowering documents is a charter drafted by the senior management team that outlines management's objectives for the proposed project and lays out in unambiguous terms the constraints within which the delivery team will operate (Exhibit 5-6). An initial draft charter is negotiated much like a contract between the delivery team and senior management. If well crafted, it establishes the accountability ground rules for the team. The team can then operate on the assumption that senior management, as a team, will fully support the execution of the process as long as it falls within the prescribed boundaries.

One of the strongest advocates of the charter as a best practice is Hans Hjort, a cofounder of the Ohio-based consulting

Exhibit 5-6. Chartering a team.

PRODUCT DEVELOPMENT DELIVERY TEAM

CUSTOMERS		CORE	SUPPLIERS	
External	Internal		Internal	External
	Management			Competencies			

Charter

1. Vision and strategy
2. Project goals
3. Market segments and competitors
4. Milestones
5. Deliverables
6. Constraints

company Innovata. In his view, six elements constitute a full-blown charter:

1. Reasons for a project and its links to the firm's vision and strategy
2. Specific project goals expressed strategically and in dollars-and-cents objectives
3. The context of the project by market segments being attacked, competitors who need to be accounted for, technologies, and other external factors that will affect the project
4. Project process ground rules for management review at milestone checkpoints or gates
5. A precise definition of expected deliverables
6. Constraints that may affect the project, such as management assumptions, resource availability, and budgetary limits

Hjort attributes the effective use of a charter to explain Volvo's development of an electric concept car in record time. "Because everybody had played a role in agreeing to the goals, they knew exactly what they were working towards," he explained. By spelling out in advance the purpose of the project and the ground rules for its development, the project team felt free to exert its judgment and act without confusion, interference, or false starts.

> The creation of a charter requires both clarity of expectations and precision of objectives from management.

The creation of a charter requires both clarity of expectations and precision of objectives from management. It thereby diminishes the likelihood of a delivery team's moving in the wrong direction. Additionally, the charter is a significant element of a team-based reward system because it spells out precise objectives against which actual performance can be measured.

4. Concurrency Redefines the Timing and the Quality of Teaming Relationships

The definition of concurrent engineering crafted by the Institute for Defense Analyses (IDA) in 1988 is strikingly similar to what we have already described as a horizontally managed strategic process: taking into account all elements of the product development cycle from idea to disposal. The important teaming feature of concurrent product development, the term used by Boeing and Honeywell to express such a nonserialized integrated approach, is the early involvement in the process by downstream players. Thus, manufacturing or distribution specialists, who may traditionally come into the picture only much later, become integral members of the core or extended team from the start. The practice of bringing downstream players early into the delivery team meets one of the design principles of delivering the whole enterprise to the customer. Concurrency must be endorsed by the senior process team as a way of doing business so as to avoid political turf fights later on.

Improved communication is a vital adjunct of concurrently managed activity. Without it, activities would be carried out like proverbial ships passing in the night. Facilitating communication is the reason why much of the DOD-funded effort in concurrent engineering is aimed at achieving seamless electronic transfer of documents and files between members of development teams: contractors, their vendors, and the client.

5. Colocation (Real and Virtual) Maximizes the Opportunity for Face-to-Face Contact to Take Place

Colocation, a core feature of successful teaming, is achieved by sitting individuals next to one another or by doing it virtually with electronic support tools. Colocated teams can be as large as Boeing's and its huge 777 aircraft development program with 225 cross-disciplinary teams and Chrysler's single car platform team of 700 or more engineers interacting together on one open floor, or as small as six to ten people in such firms as Berg Electronics, a leader in designing connectors for electronic devices, or Mitel, a maker of telephone exchanges, in Wales. In each case colocation is seen as the key to engage team members in face-to-face communication and problem solving. In most cases it means literally pulling down the ubiquitous office partitions. "There is nothing like hearing what your neighbor is saying on the phone or two or three people debating an idea nearby," said one engineer at Boeing. "It's infectious." Berg Electronics attributes colocation to its rapid reduction of product development cycles from 40 weeks to 4. "We put everyone in one room, linked them together with a computer-assisted design system, and it worked," says Tom Lyons, a site director. The downside is a lack of privacy or a desire for contact with specialists in one's area of competence.

Chrysler's move away from housing specialized skills in dispersed buildings may be the most dramatic example of large-scale investment in colocation at a single site; more than 700 colocated individuals work on a single platform. When the work load begins to taper, many are moved to a new platform project on the same floor. Also, each wing of the futuristic Tech Center houses a specialized competence that supports colocated platform teams in the open-space central areas. Individual team members return periodically to the competency relevant to them.

Colocation fulfills the do-loop principle of maximizing the opportunity for communication and information sharing. Creating colocated teams is not always easy. Even teams as small as the one at Berg Electronics required some members to relocate temporarily away from their families. At Boeing, many engineers were asked to relocate to Seattle from sites as far away as Wichita Falls. Disruption of family life can make such geographic dislocations difficult. In such cases, electronic networking is becoming an increasingly common solution in IBM, Digital, KPMG-Peat Marwick, Levi Strauss, and many other firms. Ford Motor Company "colocated" a worldwide design team by electronically linking groups in several countries together when formulating the Mondeo, its first true "world car."

A study completed some years ago at MIT noted a geometric correlation between distance and communication: The greater the separation, the worse the communication—as one of us found out at a meeting of a team of computer specialists in a large engineering center of a Big Three automotive company. As the 15 or so participants filtered into the room, the engineers sat at one end of a long table in blue jeans, their shirt pockets bearing ubiquitous floppy plastic pen holders. The head office executives sat at the other end in suits and ties. These were all employees of the same company, but they came from two distinct locations and brought with them two different languages and two radically opposed computer philosophies. Nothing constructive came of this meeting.

6. Training in Group Skills and Information Sharing Is Essential for Individuals to Interact Successfully in Teams

For strategic process management and the teaming effort it embodies to succeed, senior management must learn new skills and tools and train subordinates in their use. Anything less signals to the lower levels of the company that senior management does not consider the training important. Training, delivered by managers themselves as a top-down cascading process, is on our list of best practices. Companies such as Xerox and Federal Express have used cascading programs for many years. In both, senior executives believe that the training stuck with their employees far more effectively than had they turned to staff professionals or outside consultants.

One example of a cascading approach is a six-day course developed by the Center for Quality Management in Cambridge, Massachusetts. Serving a membership of about 40 companies, this CEO-originated center devised the course to teach the fundamentals of structured problem solving to senior executives and those who report to them. Packaged into three two-day segments, the course not only engages the participants in hands-on learning exercises but requires that what is learned be applied immediately and reported at the next two-day session. In addition, the course favors using senior executives as teachers of their peers in the course and of their subordinates in their home companies.

Ford applied a similar philosophy when it embraced the quality movement early in the 1980s. CEO Donald Petersen's attendance in basic statistical process control classes signaled to the whole company that this was a training process of strategic importance to the firm. If the boss was doing it, they probably should want to do it too. This effort quickly evolved into a vast corporate total quality training process affecting almost all of the company's 300,000 employees. And from it sprang the American Supplier Institute as an educational center to help its large supplier base.

Strategic process teaming reflects new concepts of corporate hierarchy. Process teams, unlike committees, are not just accountable for results but are collective owners of valuable know-how. The focus is less on compartmentalizing through command and control and more on unifying corporate activity through process teams. Put differently, it is the greater whole of the team that becomes an asset and not the mere sum of the individual units.

Notes

1. Steven Wheelwright, "Senior Management's Role in Changing the Process" (presentation to the International Conference of the Product Development Management Association, Boston, November 11, 1994).

2. Jon R. Katzenbach and Douglas Smith, *The Wisdom of Teams* (Boston: Harvard Business Press, 1993).

3. Kenji Kurogane, ed., *Cross-Functional Management: Principles and Practical Applications* (Tokyo: Asian Productivity Center, 1993), p. 42.

Chapter 6
Four-Fields Process Mapping

Mooka-City is a long commuter train ride from Tokyo. A small town, it is home to one of Komatsu's large tractor plants. In 1984, one of us accompanied a Japanese quality professor and consultant, Yoshi Tsuda, on one of his working visits to check on the company's progress applying total quality techniques to the product development process. On this occasion, the day was to be spent grilling the plant's 25-person management team on problems they had identified in developing a new tractor transmission.

Immediately striking to the foreign visitor was that plant managers and shop floor workers were discussing day-to-day product development issues as a cohesive team. They sat around a large square-shaped table and engaged in discussion that made clear the responsibility each shared for the issue at hand. Purchasing activities and supplier problems, inadequate standards causing undetected defects, and prototyping methods were discussed and dissected. Professor Tsuda prodded and pushed. "You must come up with more methods," he advised. "Create a large base of ideas and then discuss the merits and demerits of each." Issues were fielded without establishing blame but seeking systemic causes.

The day concluded in a meeting with Mukai Hideo, the plant manager. The conversation turned to ways in which teams can be encouraged to work cohesively. "It took us a long time," he volunteered. As he talked about the more than two decades of corporate improvement efforts deployed down into the plants, he pulled a single sheet of paper from a folder and laid it on the table. "Our whole product development process is described on this single sheet," he explained. "Everyone knows exactly what needs to be done and when." This single sheet, which he described as a quality assurance chart, showed what looked like a process flowchart but clearly contained much more information. It did not resemble anything used in the standard American program management tool kit of Gantt charts, PERT-CPM, or flow diagrams. Without fully comprehending the value or contents of this single sheet, the author brought it back to the United States.

> A single sheet of paper visually summarized a full product development cycle and all the key interactions necessary to carry it out.

It took some time for the importance of this sheet of paper to strike a cord. Its strength was in visually summarizing a full product development cycle and all the key interactions necessary to carry it out. Four process elements were integrated:

1. Individual team members
2. Phases and milestones decision points
3. Key reviews and major tasks showing the cross-organization involvement of the team members
4. Key documents necessary for the control of any single event or activity depicted

Only the essential features of the process were shown on this sheet of paper, but other sheets might be used to detail some aspect of the process. This is very different from the thick three-ring binder common to almost all big companies whose pages laboriously describe corporate procedures for product development processes. In our experience, almost all employees pay lip-service to them and then go around the system to get things done. The reason is that "the book" never quite responds to the actual circumstances faced by a project team.

In sharp contrast, the single sheet at Komatsu was a systemic representation of an entire product development process.

Renamed by one of us *four-fields maps,* they have since been introduced to numerous U.S. and European firms.[1]

> The four-fields map is the visual representation of the process a team has agreed to follow, often expressed as a plan-do-check-act sequence.

Because the planning of a process map requires intense interaction among members of the core team, it is a useful technique for establishing and recording shared goals and a common language. The four-fields map is a visual representation of the process a team has agreed to follow, often expressed in a plan-do-check-act sequence. It depicts those things that must be performed or anticipated (such as a particular test) to avoid failure. It indicates too the degree of involvement expected of downstream members who may have distribution or service responsibilities that must be known early so as to influence the product design.

As Exhibit 6-1 shows, team members are arrayed at the top. The creation of a charter is noted and placed below the individual (or group) issuing it. The charter specifies the goals and expectations for the project team. In this case, the originator of the charter is labeled as a customer since the core team will be working to fulfill the requirements laid out in the charter.

Originated by Toyota and Komatsu during the 1960s, a four-fields process map integrates four elements into a single cohesive and systemic picture of a process (see Exhibit 6-2):

1. The right combination of *team members* (core plus extended)
2. The *stages with major milestones*
3. The collaborative quality of *tasks or meetings*
4. The discipline and consistency to be applied through *guidelines, standards, requirements, or regulations* governing relationships and decisions to be made

On a single map, the principal features of a complex process—major decision points, critical reviews, key tasks—can be

Exhibit 6-1. The four-fields map.

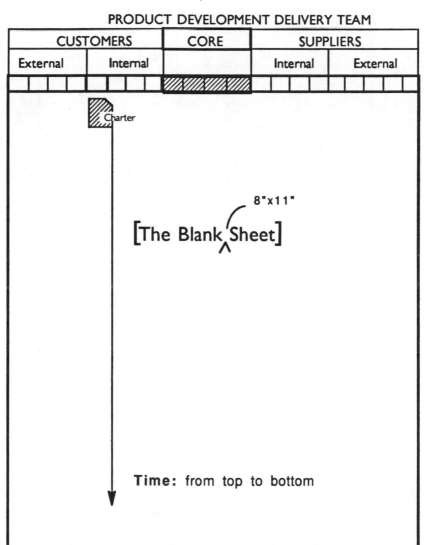

depicted and communicated with no more than 25 to 35 entries. In each case the participants in each of these tasks and events is shown.

A high-level four-fields map might show 5 or 6 milestones and 10 to 20 relationships expressed as single tasks (e.g., "collect

Exhibit 6-2. The four elements of a four-fields map.

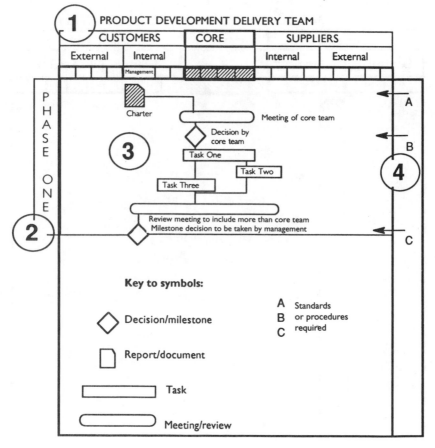

competitor information" or "prepare first prototype"). Each task is represented in such a way that those who are involved are identified. And most often more information must be shared between more than one team member in order to accomplish the task effectively. Similarly, if reviews are called for, the participants in the review are visually depicted. Finally, a process map will include references to required standards, guidelines, or regulations affecting the performance of a task, a review, or a decision. These are generally noted in the right-hand column with a reference to a method or procedure document.

A Tiered Mapping Process

Once an overall process is mapped on an $8^1/_2$ by 11 sheet, the project team may choose to focus on a single critical activity (e.g., product definition) and break it down in a similar four-fields format at one level lower in detail:

Highest level **All major project phases [the system's view]**
Milestone and reviews
Key collaborative tasks
Decisions

Next level **A grouping of tasks [Example: Product defini-tion phase]**
Key steps and reviews
Key tasks
Decisions

Next level **A single task [Example: Capture voice of cus-tomer]**
Methods and techniques
Steps to follow

In this fashion, a team can move from a systemic high-level forest view to single trees within the forest.

Preparing these maps is quick and easy; a full map can be created by a core team in two to four hours. And in a business world used to graphs and diagrams as ways of summarizing complex patterns of data distribution, four-fields maps are a uniquely useful visual shorthand for understanding and managing complex process relationships.

Four-fields maps are a uniquely useful visual shorthand for understanding and managing complex process relationships.

When a complex activity is mapped from beginning to end, a project team can more easily assume control, and its members thus become mutually accountable for their actions, a condition highlighted by consultant and author Jay Katzenbach as critical to effective teaming. "Groups that lack mutual accountability for performance," he writes, "have not shaped a common purpose and approach that can sustain them as a team."[2] Given that authority and accountability go hand in hand, more authority equals more accountability, and vice versa.

Four-Fields Applications

Boeing

One of us introduced the four-fields technique to Boeing for use in its new-aircraft program. Committed to designing the 777 without paper drawings or an initial wooden mock-up, Boeing leaders understood that close collaboration and work coordination between engineers on design-build teams (DBTs) was essential because the project would encompass more than 225 DBTs eventually. The program directors saw four-fields process mapping as a more effective means of mapping collaborative interactions than their normal procedure, which relied heavily on time-based Gantt charts.

The first pilot DBT, responsible for designing the aircraft nose, the heart of the plane with all the vital electronic controls, used process mapping to deliberate the interrelationships and phasing of work. As the members deliberated, it soon became evident that a new three-dimensional computer system used to design the whole aircraft would permit far more detailed analyses and modeling capabilities than paper drawing ever allowed, yet no one had defined what "detailed" meant. The team realized how hard it would be to specify the output of a design step if they could not specify how detailed it should be.

Using the four-fields framework as a guide, the team members identified 11 development phases spanning the four-year effort and over two weeks of meetings hammered out exit criteria for each phase. This forced the team members to communicate their needs—needs that normally would have gone unvoiced and would have been resolved later through rework and redesign. The team soon established eight possible levels of detail, each requiring different inputs and each describing different technical characteristics. This effort generated a common language understandable to each of the engineering disciplines on the team, a breakthrough given that prior paper-based drawings had only three levels of detail: a crude stick drawing, a schematic, and a final three-dimensional representation. Equipped with a shared language, they quickly agreed to common deliverables at key phase gates; for example, a hydraulic system for landing gear depicted as a level 1 detail would serve to resolve a crude layout in a portion of the aircraft.

Having to map the process forced the team members to communicate their needs—needs that normally would have gone unvoiced and would have been resolved through rework and redesign.

A map soon emerged first as large self-stick removable notes on a 20-foot-long wall and then as an orderly display of key events and interactions on a single cover sheet and more detailed ones for each of the 11 phases. One member called it the "best planning I've seen in my years here." By focusing on the mapping, the team members achieved a level of communication rarely seen in projects that in the past were managed as sequential tasks with formal hand-offs as the only juncture between one task and another. The mapping procedure had structured the discussion and provided a simple means of recording the essential features of the concurrent development process. This done, schedulers were able to construct time lines for single tasks and events.

Trane Company

The Trane Company, a maker of home and industrial air-conditioners, had much the same experience. A team of eight program managers and a group vice president spent several days laboring over the process they followed in managing new projects. One outcome was the creation of a four-fields map that for the first time documented the process. It highlighted the importance of having experienced and knowledgeable program managers to carry out projects and showed that no one in the corporation had ever before captured that experience in a way that made it replicable and usable to someone else. The mapping exercise developed a common vocabulary for managing the product development across various divisions and for sharing know-how more meaningfully.

Digital Equipment Corporation

Digital had long prided itself as a team-driven company, but by the mid- to late-1980s, it had failed to keep up with the phenomenally rapid pace of change in computers and networks. Teams took too long to develop ideas, customer input was often weak at best, and functional chimneys played more and more of a role in defining responsibilities. These difficulties bothered Michael Kleeman, a young lead engineer at Digital with project management responsibilities who saw no reason that the teams he led could not achieve $5\times$ to $10\times$ improvements. One of the best ways to achieve this, he argued, was through discussion and clear agreement on process mechanics at the very start of a project.

> Often a simple question will unleash a lengthy debate in which it is evident, but always too late, that everyone has a substantially different definition of something.

"I've seen people come into a room all believing that everyone else is in sync," Kleeman states. "But often a simple question will unleash a lengthy debate in which it is evident, but always too late, that everyone has a substantially different definition of something." Exactly that happened in a meeting one of us facilitated. The eight-person team had just agreed to include a review step focused on evaluating a "soft model" of a design—but it turned out that no one on the team agreed on what a "soft model" meant. Some thought it was a three-dimensional design developed on a computer-aided design system. Some

Exhibit 6-3. A full example of a four-fields map.

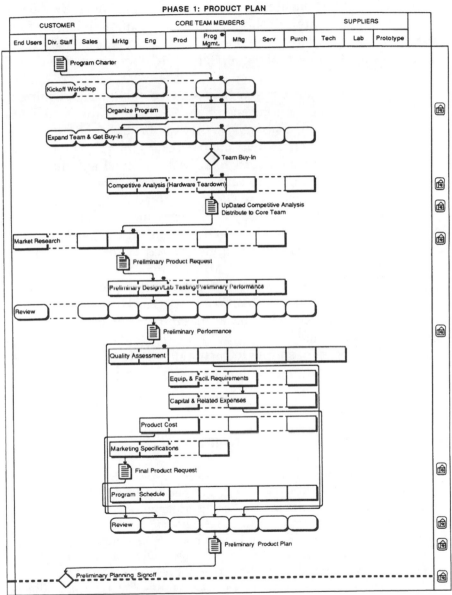

Note: This map was drafted by using Team/flow™ software, which allows documents to be tagged to process symbols and thus retrieved from wherever they reside in a network. Team/flow was originally developed under the name CFM/pro by TSG, the firm of one coauthor.

thought it was a simple model made out of Styrofoam to indicate spatial relationships: a disc here, the motor here, the board
there. Others thought it should be a stiff metal model. "Just that
agreement on what a soft model meant probably saved us a
week of time for each of eight people," Kleeman concluded.

Early and intense interaction is a vital step in establishing a
common language among members of a core team—and later
with suppliers and customers as they are brought into the process. In support, the four-fields map becomes the visual representation of the team members' relationships and the boundaries
within which they agree to carry out their mission.

For management, these maps, as noted in Exhibit 6-3, are
the starting point for do-loop teams to plan their collaboration.
They can be exhibited in enlarged formats on team room walls,
faxed with handwritten notations, shared with new teams to
give them a running start. At Mitel, a maker of telephone exchange systems, the company's Welsh division posts these maps
on the walls of colocated team workspaces. They serve as a re-
minder of the process they have agreed to follow and as a guide
to follow-on teams.

The technique, simple to carry out, meets the best-practice
requirement of helping develop a systemic perspective of a complex set of tasks.

Notes

1. Dan Dimancescu, *The Seamless Enterprise, Making Cross-Functional Management Work* (New York: Harper/Business, 1992). They are
described in further detail in Kenji Kurogane, ed., *Cross-Functional
Management: Principles and Practical Applications* (Tokyo: Asia Productivity Organization, 1993), and K. Uchimaru, S. Okamoto, and B. Kurahara, *TQM for Technical Groups: Total Quality Principles for Product
Development* (Portland, Ore.: Productivity Press, 1993).

2. Jay R. Katzenbach and Douglas Smith, *The Wisdom of Teams*
(Boston: Harvard Business Press, 1993), p. 61.

Chapter 7
A System of Metrics

You get what you measure.

The mark of a world-class product company is its ability to replicate successes and to improve performance constantly. Having a comprehensive system of metrics to measure performance, particularly if the goal is 5× and 10× improvements consistently over time, is essential. Building a system of process metrics means translating objectives into well-targeted and measurable actions that can be used to improve a company's performance. The senior management team must select well-targeted performance objectives and not get lost in a forest of measures that dilute a team's energy and focus.

In the late 1980s, when one of us started benchmarking how the world's best companies manage their product development process, none of the 12 companies that participated measured the quality of the process itself. It was not viewed as a priority; after all, no one was responsible for it. These companies understood that measuring the quality of the product was important, but none had a methodology for measuring the quality of the process.

A metric is a quantifiable characteristic one can manage against.

Measures and metrics: the semantic distinction is important. Art Schneiderman, vice president of quality at Analog Devices and now an independent consultant, offers a useful way of characterizing the difference: "Measurement applies to anything that has a quantifiable characteristic. A metric, on the other hand, is a quantifiable characteristic one can manage against."[1] Knowing that 260 million Americans live in the United States is a *measurement*. Knowing that 60 percent of shipments are going out late is a *metric* one can "manage against" by planning a set of actions and remedies to ameliorate the outcome.

The tangible quality of a number is attractive in a results-driven world. That's why *metrics* is a magic word with most managers. It helps to focus improvement efforts and to provide feedback, guides recognition or rewards, and quantifies a measure of product development effectiveness. Truly effective metrics are elusive, yet we have distinguished three types that together constitute a systemic approach to process measurement.

Three Types of Metrics

Static Measures: The Results Scorecard

Static metrics are measurements of results gathered only after an event has occurred—for example, sales revenue or market share. Because there is a long lag between the event and the measurement, it is impossible to take any corrective action. Indeed, such measures are often the only ones a product development management team looks at—and only after the team has finished its work and disbanded. Other long-cycle static metrics include mean time between failure or actual service costs against planned service costs.

But static metrics are only one component of a process-focused system of measurement. Results-focused measures such as profitability, market share, or return on investment may be meaningful from a business perspective but offer little motivation to someone down in the trenches working on a product development team and even less to someone lower in the organization. Only when business objectives, or what is sometimes referred to as the enterprise scorecard, are meaningfully translated do the metrics become meaningful to delivery teams. One way

to translate results objectives into metrics is to identify performance gaps.

Motivational Metrics: Half-Life Performance Gaps

This category of metrics, still not fully understood or widely
implemented in the business world, is the key to translating
business objectives into meaningful and motivating measures
that delivery teams can work against.

It is clear that leading companies—Motorola is a good example—target 5× to 10× improvements and manage to achieve
them consistently over long periods of time. Multiples of this
sort do not mean increments in static measures such as profitability or market share. A large company cannot sustain such
growth rates. A more useful way to think of 5× or 10× improvements is in terms of gaps that need closing. For example,
if we were to measure the time required to deliver a product to
a customer—6 weeks, let's say—against the theoretically possible—perhaps 2 weeks—the difference of 4 weeks is the performance gap. Similarly, if a firm delivers on time 82 percent of the
time and 99 percent on time is theoretically possible within
known constraints, the real gap to be managed is 17 percentage
points wide. We can now talk in terms of 5× or 10× improvements over a predetermined time period. This is exactly what
George Fisher did when he left Motorola as its chairman and
CEO and took on the chairmanship of Eastman Kodak. Improvements by factors of ten became the mandate from the top down.

In a world of sophisticated and complex systems and organizations, reducing even seemingly small gaps can have significant impacts if reduced by factors of five to ten. This is well
known in the world of manufacturing. A copying machine, for
example, is a system made up of three principal elements: mechanical components with moving parts, the reprographic technology that transfers the image onto the paper copy, and
electronics (hardware and software) that control the system.
These three elements have to interact flawlessly over long periods of time. If each of the three systems is only 98 percent efficient, the whole system will break down 6 percent of the time—a
wholly unacceptable standard of performance. The aim is to re-

duce variability and the range of error to parts per million from the start. Carefully executed product development minimizes such error through good design and scrupulous understanding of downstream needs such as manufacturing, delivery, and servicing.

Problems: Small but Deadly

At another company,

> A problem with [a very small component] electric capacitors, could cause some of its notebook computers for European markets to fail when plugged into certain European voltages. . . . The reason, it appears, was an earlier problem with the machines . . . which prevented them from recognizing more than 16 bytes of RAM. . . . Glitches such as these coupled with seriously delayed notebook product cycles may be hurting the company already. [It] has slipped to a distant second place behind [Company Y] with which it was tied earlier.[2]

Consider problems in electronic systems that have hundreds upon hundreds, if not thousands, of computer chips. The world defect standard for welding leads of computer chips onto computer boards is now measured in parts per billion, a standard in companies such as NEC. However, when we visited a European maker of telephone switching systems that contain numerous computer boards, the defect rate was proudly touted as "world class" at 250 per million welds executed, almost 1,000 times *worse* than NEC's standard. How can a company such as this maintain credibility with its customers? Conversations with managers revealed that the company maintains a large and costly service staff to keep periodic equipment breakdowns from halting telephone service caused by defects in the boards it manufactures.

Discovering Improvement "Half-Lives"

Art Schneiderman, when serving as vice president for quality at Analog Devices in 1987, made a discovery during a long air trip from Tokyo to Boston that led him to understand how best to manage $10\times$ improvements. Over the course of the 14-hour flight, he thumbed through quality practice documents gathered during his visit. One, in particular, caught his fancy—a chart from Yokogawa-Hewlett-Packard, Ltd. showing improvements in the dip soldering process on computer boards measured over a ten-year period. That the improvements in failure rates went from excellent to superior was impressive. But something else struck Art: a distinct and predictable pattern to the steep downward improvement curve.

He took a blank piece of paper and drew horizontal logarithmic lines thinner and thinner in spacing. Then he replotted the Yokogawa data and found the data plotted as a pure straight line showing the company consistently improving the dip soldering defect rate *by 50 percent every three months*. The consistency with which this was plotted struck him as truly significant.

Back at work he and his staff gathered information from varied industry publications on about a hundred widely diverse activities—from errors in purchasing orders, to scrap and repair costs, to accounting miscodes—and their improvement rates in various companies. To his surprise they all came out shaped much like the Yokogawa curve: 50 percent improvements over uniform periods of time. The length of the period, they discovered, depended on two factors: the technical complexity of the activity and the complexity of the organizational effort required to carry it out.

Art termed what he saw *half-life metrics,* or the time required to achieve 50 percent reductions in a performance gap. It was evident to Art, being well versed in quality practices, that it is easier to diagnose the root cause of a weakness (a performance gap) and therefore attack it than to determine how to increase a strength. Based on this research, Art and his team put together a small matrix indicating expected half-life values for activities of varying degrees of complexity (Exhibit 7-1). By this formula, achieving 50 percent reduction in a performance gap of the simplest activity would take one month. The most complex project, such as closing a time-to-market gap in product development process, might take 22 months. In Art Schneiderman's words,

Exhibit 7-1. Expected half-life values and complexity.

		Half-Life [in months]		
		Technical Complexity		
	High	14	18	22
Organization	**Medium**	7	9	11
Complexity	**Low**	1	3	5
		Low	**Medium**	**High**

Source: Arthur Schneiderman.

the half-life metric suddenly focused the "team on the intended improvement result and a realistic time frame within which to achieve it." Narrowing the right performance gaps would meet the business objectives of the enterprise. These gaps proved a serendipitous translation of objectives into measures that delivery teams could work against—hence, the motivational aspect that was otherwise missing. Colloquially it meant, "We can do that. Let's get started."

> A natural impulse was to take a competitor's capability as the outer limit. But this would mean playing endless catch-up because the competitor would also be moving toward a new target value.

Art took the measurement of a gap a step further. A natural impulse was to take a competitor's capability as the outer limit. But this would mean playing endless catch-up because the competitor would also be moving toward a new target value. Instead he established a theoretical outer limit under current constraints and know-how, yielding a vital long-term line of sight and the "half-life" increments necessary to get closer and closer to the limits. "Without it," he says, "one is left floating, not knowing what the shape of the real half-life curve looks like." The goal is to know the shape of that curve and to get on it, much as a surfer might get on a wave. One can easily project ten years forward.

If the improvement rate is not rapid enough, a break-through is needed. When this occurs, the slope of the curve can be reshaped, thereby forcing the competition into a catch-up position. This is central to a $10\times$ view of managing a metric, and it was just what Calsonic's Llanelli Radiator Division in Wales did. It replaced old-fashioned hand-braised copper coils in its car radiators with almost fully automatic braised aluminum technology requiring almost no hand labor. By virtue of this one step, the organization produces a cheaper, lighter, and better-performing radiator. Sales to the European automotive market shot up from 2 percent of market share to 16 percent in four years. The company is now poised to sustain continued improvement on its new and steeper performance gap curve.

> There is nothing worse than creating an expectation that cannot be realized.

"In all this," says Art Schneiderman, "it is vital that the time for the half-life improvement be realistic. There is nothing worse than creating an expectation that cannot be realized." Teams are quickly demoralized and management is quick to place blame. Therefore the senior process team is responsible for translating business results into meaningful performance gaps and to recalibrate the metrics continuously against competitive and new technological data.

Analog Devices applied the half-life system of metrics across its nine worldwide plants, with amazing effects. Using data gathered from 21 customer companies, it determined that it could achieve half-life improvement in late deliveries every nine months. In other words, it would take nine months to reduce the current late-delivery rate by 50 percent. More complex lot rejects, Schneiderman determined, would take 15.5 months to reduce by 50 percent. Using such measures as a guide to managing improvements, the company's performance jumped significantly. By 1990, within a four-year period, the company was declared the midsize semiconductor Supplier of the Year by Dataquest.

Applying Half-Life Metrics to Product Development

The half-life can be applied to the product development process. A key example—one that plagues many companies and which we describe in this book—is the rate of change orders or errors measured during the development of a product. Given that design errors cost a company geometrically more to correct the closer one gets to production day, it is critical that the rate be controlled and reduced.

Two basic types of errors occur during product development: conformance errors, which originate with mistakes or miscalculations that keep a design from working as expected, and user requirement errors, which occur when the design fails to meet a user requirement. Both types cause delays and additional cost, and they eat up valuable time. Few companies have a firm handle on managing the wasted effort and elapsed time spent on error corrections. In both cases, the hope is for errors to peak early in the product development cycle and then quickly ramp down to zero on the day of production.

Making gap reduction an objective during the product development cycle will have immediate and measurable bearing in almost every case on the cost of the project, the cycle time, and the quality of the output delivered to a customer.

A team bent on continuous improvement seeks to target such error rates by correctly assessing the size of the gap and aggressively managing its reduction. They can estimate the time required to reduce an error rate by 50 percent. Making gap reduction an objective during the product development cycle will have immediate and measurable bearing in almost every case on the cost of the project, the cycle time, and the quality of the output delivered to a customer. These are all bottom-line results that affect market share and profitability. Reduction of error rates also releases valuable skilled talent to work on new projects far sooner.

An example from the Raytheon Corporation illustrates the direct correlation between the narrowing of a strategically important performance gap over a six-year period—in this case, the cost of software rework and productivity increases (Exhibit 7-2).

Establishing the size and time frame for a performance gap allows a company to strategize whether breakthroughs or steady incremental improvements are most appropriate. For the Japanese automobile parts maker Nippon Denso, this is viewed as a vital planning step in defining radical breakthroughs necessary to remain competitive. "In setting targets for the radiator design, for example, the Nippondenso team graphed performance-to-weight ratios of radiators built during the past several decades. They then projected this data and set targets to beat the competition in the next decade, which required a 50 percent reduction in radiator weight."[3]

The task of a senior strategic process team, at the executive level, is to prioritize gaps that need addressing. A well-chosen gap will have systemic benefits measured in increased profitability and market share. The gap is then deployed by requiring that a product development team reduce it by a specified factor. This goal, spelled out in the team's charter, will generally include acknowledgment of the cost to attack it. In one company's copy products division, the problem was average defects per unit at final test. To close the gap, the half-life was determined to be 7.8 months. This rate of improvement was maintained for 40 months, or about five half-life cycles. At the time we last looked, defects had been reduced by more than 95 percent.

Teams seeking to make $5\times$ and $10\times$ type improvements must be able to assess root causes and arrive at remedies expeditiously. Given the weakness orientation of the gap, root cause analysis is the key to identifying the highest-leverage corrective actions. Thus, having a disciplined analytical methodology such

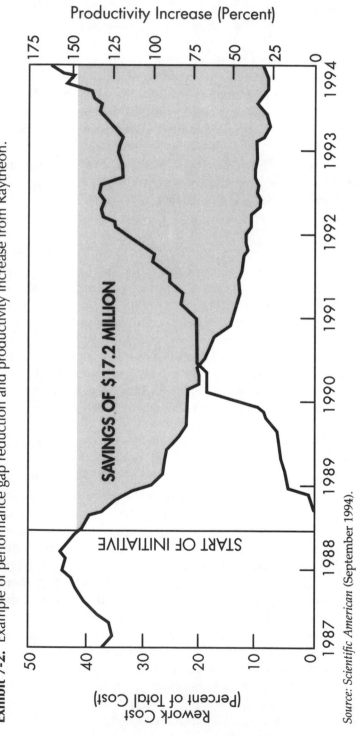

Exhibit 7-2. Example of performance gap reduction and productivity increase from Raytheon.

Source: Scientific American (September 1994).

as the standard seven-step structured problem-solving technique is vital to the management of half-life metrics by teams.

> Having a disciplined analytical methodology such as the standard seven-step structured problem-solving technique is vital to the management of half-life metrics.

NEC put a major emphasis on improving its problem anticipation rate in the mid-1980s. It took a structured problem-solving approach, which was instrumental to achieving $5\times$ and $10\times$ improvement rates. The metric it attached to an improvement rate was computed as follows:

$$\text{Problem anticipation rate} = \frac{\text{Number anticipated} \times 100\%}{\text{Number anticipated} + \text{Number not anticipated}}$$

From 1985 to 1987, delivery teams drove the problem anticipation rates for PC software from approximately 25 percent to almost 100 percent, for microcomputer systems from 10 percent to over 50 percent, and for microcomputer modules from just under 60 percent to about 65 percent.

Dynamic Metrics: Action Focused

The third category of metrics is dynamic with real-time data feedback as a goal. By doing root-cause analyses of performance gaps, teams can target short-term goals and closely monitor their ability to reach them. Metrics associated with targeted goals can be used to predict the probable outcome of work in process. Because they indicate immediate diversions from a target value, they allow a team to take corrective action. Statistical process control charts are a widely used example of a real-time dynamic metric. One can manage against them and thus make continuous incremental improvements that are the core of total quality best practice. Other dynamic metrics that could be identified and prioritized include numbers of reviews carried out, number of customers interviewed, ratio of professional skills on a development team, or the ratio of hours spent correcting bugs and total time spent on a software development project.

The ideal predictive metric should provide quick feedback and have low complexity.

"The ideal predictive metric should provide quick feedback and have low complexity," says John Carter, a leader in applying predictive measures to product development.[4] An example is the simple measurement of the actual number of customers interviewed against the number planned. The data are immediately visible. If an insufficient number have been interviewed, it can be assumed that user needs are inadequately assessed, and corrective action can be taken immediately.

At Fujitsu's mainframe development group in Japan, one of the predictive methods of measuring design quality is the number of large-scale integrated circuit (LSI) design remakes. (A remake is a design change made to correct a design error or to meet a specific user requirement.) Fujitsu uses as a metric the total number of remakes divided by the total number of LSIs. If there are 500 LSIs in a system and 500 remakes, which is the norm, the result is multiplied by 100 percent. Particularly good results would be 50 percent, and particularly bad results would be 150 to 200 percent. This simple predictive measure tells a team and its managers fast and easily whether they are on a planned course; if they are not, they can immediately adjust their process.

A predictive measure tells a team and its managers fast and easily whether they are on a planned course; if they are not, they can immediately adjust their process.

The Information Systems Group at Fujitsu, which is responsible for developing the full mainframe systems, agrees in advance with the Semiconductor Group, which creates the LSI designs, on a financial penalty based on the number of remakes required. Built into the price to be paid by the Information Systems Group is one remake per LSI. The penalty increases as the number of remakes increases and also reflects the number of weeks after release of the final specifications that the revision is made. If it is prior to two weeks after release, there is no charge.

Releases or approvals by the Information Systems Group to their supplier divisions normally begin halfway through the design verification stage. Three key metrics guide their decision to approve a release:

1. The number of design bugs found before data release, after data release, and during systems test
2. The number of remakes of LSI
3. The number of remakes of printed circuit boards

The number of bugs identified (Metric 1) are plotted over time, with separate plot lines for the instruction unit, the storage control unit, and the execution unit. From years of experience and data gathering, Fujitsu knows the shape (that is, the number of cumulative bugs at any given point) these curves should take during the design verification process. With an anticipated number of bugs as a standard, Fujitsu can track in real time the actual bugs detected against the standard. The degree of risk is managed by watching the development and shape of the bug curves. If they follow the expected curve, everything is fine, and release dates can be planned. If they are better than expected, the release date can be accelerated. And if worse, special corrective attention is applied to the process to bring it back in line. In this manner, dynamic metrics are used to halt, slow, or accelerate the process as needed. Because the metrics are predictive, extra resources can be applied early when it is much more cost-effective to correct errors than far down the production cycle.

Limitations of Metrics

Measures have two inherent pitfalls. First, over time people will learn how to beat the system. Almost any metric can be abused when people learn to manipulate the numbers to meet the targeted expectations. To overcome this, continuous recalibration is required by the senior process team.

> It is incumbent on senior management to recalibrate its system of measurement carefully and frequently in order to get all its strategic processes working together.

Second, even the best metrics can lead parts of an organization to overwhelm another. It is incumbent on senior management *as a team* to balance its system of measurement carefully and frequently to get all its strategic processes working together: product development, order delivery, cost control, research and development, employee training, and information systems. Managing the objectives scorecard through quarterly executive reviews is one way to do this, and using online data allows continuous monitoring. In some companies, the data are posted on terminals for all to see.

> Metrics must be designed not with independent parts as targets but with the whole system's behavior as a goal.

Dr. Michiyuki Uenohara, chief technical officer of NEC, believes that the second pitfall is the biggest danger. Measuring subprocesses separately can create disharmonies within the larger business unit or division. The ultimate success of any product, he stresses, requires that the total organization work together in achieving collective goals. Metrics must be designed not with independent parts as targets but with the whole system's behavior as a goal.

The three types of measures introduced in this chapter—static, motivational, and dynamic—offer managers, teams, and individuals a systemic approach to process management that responds to each of their needs. Later, when we discuss rewards and recognition, the importance of taking such a systemic approach rather than focusing on narrowly defined results will become clearer.

Notes

1. Arthur M. Schneiderman, "Metrics for the Order Fulfillment Process," unpublished manuscript, 1994.

2. "Problems Continue to Bedevil Compaq's LTE Elite," *Computerworld*, December 26, 1994–January 2, 1995, p. 4.

3. Allen Ward, "The Second Toyota Paradox: How Delaying Decisions Can Make Better Cars Faster," *Sloan Management Review*, Spring 1995, p. 55.

4. Presentation to the IAPD workshop on metrics, September 1991.

Chapter 8
Reviews

Kiyoshi Uchimaru belonged to a unique class of innovative hands-on managers who forged Japan's postwar boom. When he was asked in 1980 to take over a newly founded subsidiary of NEC, its primary mission was to design integrated computer chips for the parent company. By 1987, he had turned the fledgling company into a Deming Prize–winning enterprise.[1] Early in 1993, one of us spoke with him on the role of reviews in product development.

His first comments were unexpected: "Our review process is based on methods learned from NASA's PPP [phase program planning]." He was referring to the rigorous application of design reviews to the design and development of weapon systems that the Department of Defense had pioneered and that NASA would push further. More recently, the Department of the Navy published a well-crafted book on product development procedures, *Best Practices: How to Avoid Surprises in the World's Most Complicated Technical Process*.[2] The ten-page section on design reviews is succinct and useful to any enterprise. "The objective of all design reviews," it states, "is to ensure that the design will fulfill its requirements."

But under Uchimaru, the discipline of reviews was taken beyond design. As he put it, "The purpose of reviews is for prediction and prevention of errors in next steps." This is different from the DOD and NASA design review objective of making sure that the design fulfills its requirements at the moment of the review. The implications became clearer as Uchimaru quickly outlined five product development planning steps.

1. Decompose the process into its basic elements and create a project (four-fields) map.

2. Arrange reviews into a series of decision-making steps.
3. At each review step, carry out analyses of defects into more and more detailed levels and determine where the detected problems first occurred.
4. Brush up (i.e., strengthen) design review procedures to prevent reoccurrence of causes of errors.
5. Use the quality table (QFD) matrix as the basic planning tool for diagnosing and resolving problems; matrices are no bigger than 30 by 30 items on each axis.

Uchimaru described two kinds of reviews: as design and management reviews. More significant was his innovative use of "brush-up" reviews as a method of improving the product development process itself. Indeed, this step surfaced as an important clue to his rapid mastery of chip design at NEC-NIMS. Every review became an introspective session into why things were happening the way they were and not just whether the design met the requirement. The methodology he installed was designed to achieve a continuous, seamless change from formation to formation.

The purpose of reviews is for prediction and prevention of errors in next steps.

To gain better control over the improvement of the product development process, Uchimaru borrowed a clever charting concept from Toyota. Called the T-matrix, it is a systemic yet simple way of tracking errors and bugs. The middle column identifies at what step in the process the bugs and errors should have been discovered if the technical review process had been working. At the left side is noted the step at which the defect was discovered. And on the opposite side are noted (from the center out) the steps at which the bugs or defects originated. The pattern of notations indicates how well the review process is working, and the accumulation of notations to the right instantly tells the eye at which steps most of the bugs are concentrated and thus which steps need improving the next time round. The whole exercise recognizes that even the best of design reviews may not pick up all the defects.

Formal design review meetings are held frequently at NEC-NIMS. They last about an hour, and 10 to 20 people attend. The section or chief engineer chairs the meeting. Management reviews last about 4 hours, longer than in most other companies we benchmarked, and with the customer often in attendance. The first of two primary reviews is based on contracted client specifications, and the second confirms whether the contract has been fulfilled. These formal reviews are always preceded by what Uchimaru terms a *workthrough*—a team exercise to determine whether the process is working and how best to resolve detected problems.

Much like a time-out in a sports game, these workthrough techniques are the principal mechanism for fine-tuning the process as it unfolds. But Uchimaru added a twist of using the review to "return to the source." By this he meant going to where the problems originated and using reviews to perfect the process itself. He was thus able to extend the review from a NASA-styled inspection mechanism (Are we meeting requirements?) to a diagnostic one (Is the design process working as well as it should?) intended to prevent errors from happening in the next cycle.

By 1987, the system he crafted was so well oiled that integrated chip designs were being delivered correct the first time 98.9 percent of the time. This was an exceptional achievement, especially if one takes into account the increased complexity of chips during this same period.

A Tool Kit of Review Methods

A family of review types exists, categorized on one axis by technical or business purpose and on the other by the formality or informality with which they are carried out (Exhibit 8-1).

Management reviews are formal and planned. They focus on business issues and goals. They start with issues related to the customer, the customer's needs, and the marketplace, but their primary focus relates to resource management and corporate and business unit strategic direction. Issues here include product line fit, sales and payback expectations, project schedule,

Exhibit 8-1. Types of reviews.

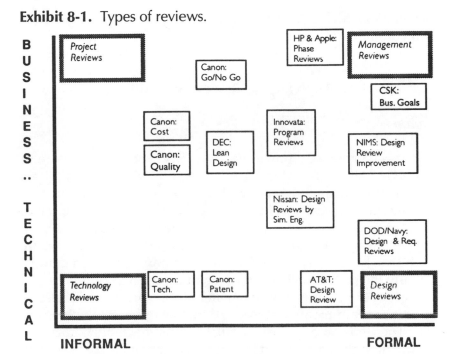

timely introduction to the market, and whether the technology is available and adequately mature to meet quality and cost targets. They are critical to maintaining corporate commitment and strategic alignment within the corporation's product lines. Management reviews usually take place in the development process when a transition occurs from one phase of the process to another—for example, from concept to product planning or development to ramp-up. The frequency of phase reviews varies widely by company and product complexity. Fuji Xerox schedules nine, AT&T five, and Apple five per product development cycle. The number of formal gates reflects points at which important resource commitments are made. Informal project reviews are carried out periodically as needed.

Design reviews are formally planned and rigorously applied. Experts in technical subjects are generally present, and the intent is to qualify the technical capability of a design. Design reviews and gate or phase reviews complement one another. Together they serve to identify and resolve both technical and business issues and problems. They maintain management's awareness and commitment.

Applying the Review Methods

Canon

Canon's copying equipment division has customized its use of reviews. The product development team holds quality reviews to evaluate the quality attained by the first engineering or trial models. It rates each defect on a scale of 1 to 10 in order to differentiate important, critical defects from smaller, easier-to-solve defects. The totals of the defect ratings provide a measure of the quality of the project. If there are many high-rated defects, usually the project will be halted pending their resolution. If the defects are primarily low-rated items, the project will receive conditional approval to proceed to the next phase.

The division also carries out technology reviews focusing on the product concept and its relation to the maturity or robustness of available technologies. The concept always takes precedence, and the goal is to identify technologies necessary to realize it. The team assisting in this review brings experts in the required technologies together with the product planning and marketing personnel who represent the customer. Through group brainstorming, the team identifies novel engineering solutions to realize the concept.

Teruo Yamanouchi of Daitobunka University, the former head of Canon's R&D Committee, sees this review procedure as an opportunity to create new, innovative ideas and product features early in the developmental process. A by-product of this type of review is a direct and important input to Canon's longer-term technology development program.

The strategic importance of patent reviews is strongly emphasized by Canon as a result of the enormous problems it had in overcoming Xerox's patent positioning in copiers. Canon has a competitive patent strategy of its own. From the beginning of a product development project, a special group, largely independent of the product development team whose work they are paralleling, examines basic and peripheral patent opportunities. It looks for patents that will defend a market position and put them on the offensive; it scans those held by other companies as well.

Professor Teruo Yamanouchi described a web of over 900 interrelated patents Canon held on its cartridge copier alone and a similar coverage on laser printers. He stressed this as a strategically important area in establishing and maintaining the company's dominance in laser printer production. A critical aspect of the patent review is that it must be completed during the period of early review and not be allowed to trail out later in the process.

All teams at one point or another are faced with deciding whether to bring a product to market on schedule with a technology they know will soon be outmoded or wait for a new technology being developed. Companies such as Sony, NEC, and Canon almost always bring the product to market on schedule as long as the technology available equals the performance of competitive products already in the market. They will add the new technology only after questions of its maturity and robustness are resolved. The reason is always the same: to minimize risk and to gain or preserve market share.

NEC's Yonazawa Laptop Plant

The laptop factory, a two-hour ride away from Tokyo, lies in a mountainous region long noted for its remoteness and independence. The entrepreneurial character of the plant's employees is occasionally attributed to this tradition. The plant, recently acquired by NEC, brought with it a spirit that may explain the extraordinary speed with which laptops are brought to market.

As the NEC case suggests, some development cycles are so fast that there is time only for technical reviews (formal and informal) at the factory. At NEC's Yonazawa factory laptop PCs generally start with 60 percent clean sheet designs, and move from commercial specification to full production in 15 weeks. The whole product development process comprises five *formal design reviews* plus informal technical reviews that may take place daily.

| Some development cycles are so fast that there is time only for technical reviews.

The five formal reviews are full team meetings expanded to include production line managers, with reporting lines going to both the factory general manager and the PC business unit. The president or general manager of the Yonazawa factory, with the development team leader, has direct and full responsibility for product cost, quality, schedule, and development budget. The business unit, in this somewhat unusual organizational structure in Japan, retains full responsibility for the larger business issues, including commercial viability.

The commercial and technical specifications for NEC's laptop computers are developed simultaneously by a subgroup of the product development team working at the business unit headquarters in Tokyo. The subgroup members are three factory-based design engineers and five persons from the business unit's market research and product planning groups. The business unit taps ongoing monitoring of markets and competitors. At the start of a new product development cycle, the latest knowledge is brought to the subgroup. It can then complete the development of both the commercial and technical specifications simultaneously in a period of a few weeks—just half the time it took when these specifications were developed and negotiated sequentially.

The first design review (Review I) concludes the simultaneous development of the technical and commercial specification and gates the start of design. It follows this agenda:

Design Review Points
- Clear definition of required conditions and confirmation of reliability
- Systems framework and design guide
- Operational and functional design guide
- Cost objectives and scheduling
- Comparison with competitors

Review Items
- Function, capability, and structure

- Past successful and unsuccessful examples
- Required quality development tables
- List of important quality parts
- Environmental and operational characteristics
- Safety and maintainability
- Reliability
- Failure modes effects test (FMEA) and fault tolerance analysis (FTA)

The focus of the design reviews, while always looking to the future and trying to identify potential problems at the earliest possible time, will advance with the phase. Design Review I focuses on clear definition of function, confirmation of technical reliability, cost objectives, comparison with competitive products, and past successful and unsuccessful examples.

Design Review II takes place prior to the construction of the engineering prototype. It expands the focus to include safety, reliability expectations, appropriateness of parts and materials, and the realization of quality and function objectives.

There are usually two iterations of the design, with the second correcting technical errors made in the first. Once the second design iteration has begun, no further changes can be initiated from outside Yonazawa. Market requirements are frozen, and new features will be held for the next cycle. Changes after the start of the second iteration are all for technical reasons. If continuing changes coming from the marketing and sales functions indicate that the marketing inputs were faulty, the project is aborted and started over.

It is toward the end of the design phase that engineering change orders peak in this state-of-the-art product development process. No hardware has been made. Errors are detected in simulation by the use of various CAD modeling techniques, including electronic simulation and stereo lithography. Engineering change orders peak at the earliest possible phase, a point at which many other companies do not even measure them. A second and lower peak is at preproduction evaluation. The laptop development teams, which have worked either together or on successive generations of laptops for an average of five years, have an enormous storehouse of captured and documented experience. Teams produce four to five models a year depending on the percentage clean sheet design.

As soon as designs and circuit diagrams are complete, they are taken to Intel and tested to verify their compatibility with Intel microprocessors. The same process takes place with manufacturers of other critical components. The schematics are similarly taken to the semiconductor division of NEC, which does the layout and returns it to Yonazawa. Yonazawa then redoes the schematic from the layout to check whether everything is correct.

Design Review II gates the development of the engineering prototype, and Design Review III follows the completion of the engineering prototype. Design Review III shifts the focus somewhat to the degree of satisfaction of functional and operational requirements and to the ease and cost of manufacturing; one thing it seeks to identify are bottleneck technologies.

Design reviews are detailed in looseleaf binders holding design review criteria for laptops. These are the repositories for team experience. They have not been written and imposed by a staff group; they are the living, changing experiences of laptop development teams.

Following the completion of Design Review III, the production preparation phase is started, which concludes with Design Review IV, the product review. This focuses on product quality and the degree to which function, safety, reliability, and maintainability have been realized.

Mass trial follows the product review and at its conclusion Design Review V, productivity evaluation, takes place. Here focus is on mass producibility, process design, process capability, quality control processes, an improvement plan for remaining technical problems, and the identification of any new technical problems. Upon successful completion of the productivity evaluation, full production starts. The time from the development planning conference that initiates the product development process to full production is three and one-half months, with 50 to 55 people involved full time—a total of just under 200 man-months.

Each design review follows a flowchart that identifies the person responsible for preparing the review, the preprevious preparation required, and the paths to follow in the case of each of the three possible outcomes: failure, conditional pass, and pass. In the case of failure, the review will start over from the preparation stage when the team is ready again. In the event of a conditional pass, there is a five-step action process terminating in a reporting conference. The final step in each design review is the organization, storage, and application of review results data. The knowledge-creating and -capturing process is a critical part of each design review.

| The final step in each design review is the organization, storage, and application of review results data. This knowledge-creating and -capturing process is a critical part of each design review.

Fuji-Xerox

Fuji Xerox had over 150 product development projects under-way in early 1993: 82 at the planning stage and 75 being carried out. The projects extended over a time horizon that reached three years ahead. Classified according to annual sales expected, these projects fall into three groups: projects with annual sales below ¥20 billion ($200 million), between ¥20 billion and ¥100 billion ($200 million to $1 billion), and above ¥100 billion.

Approval levels vary for the three categories, but both group-level and senior-level management, in addition to the business unit management, take part in the first three of a total of nine gate reviews in all three project categories: the product planning initiative review, the product development initiative review, and the product design initiative review. Group and senior management recognize that these are the most highly leveraged reviews, and they participate regardless of the size of the project.

The phase reviews at Fuji Xerox represent management control points where third-party approval is granted or withheld. There are two levels of preparation for each review. First, the team's internal working reviews determine that the activities scheduled for that phase have been successfully carried out or that they choose to enter the review with some content incomplete to receive a conditional pass. The team then prepares for the third-party review. The final review by the Program Review Committee is preceded by one week by a preliminary review by the Program Management Committee. Both of these committees are supported by the corporate functional groups: planning, finance, technology, cost management, legal, and the Product Assurance Center. Each of these supports both the Program Management and Program Review committees and signs off on the review items within its purview. The meetings of both committees take place weekly on Thursday. They are part of the corporate calendar and adhere strictly to a one-hour format. The review sequence is:

1. Product planning initiative
2. Product development initiative
3. Product design initiative
4. Production investment initiative
5. Production/marketing preparation initiative
6. Manufacturing initiative
7. Marketing initiative
8. Early working system initiative
9. Exception initiative

Each phase review is structured around 27 transfer criteria, each of which has a department or functional owner, one or more activities, and specific criteria corresponding to each activity. For example, planning is responsible at the Phase 2 transfer for three activities:

1. *Study the product family and variants* and establish (prove) that the technology required to realize them is available and proven (robust).
2. *Set the realizable design quality target* and confirm its conformance with the target established in the product concept phase.
3. *Set the unit manufacturing cost* and break it down by cost factors relating to the design quality targets (number 2).

Each review also looks ahead and reviews the resource requirements for the next phase, the action plan, and confirms the criteria for subsequent reviews.

> It is in these early reviews that senior management must ensure strategic fit and resource prioritization.

It is in these early reviews, where market and strategic alignment are ensured and customer requirements, features, product line fit, and technology requirements are established and verified, that senior management must ensure strategic fit and resource prioritization. In other companies we have benchmarked, all too frequently senior management become involved only *after* these early stages; as a result, early reviews may be carried out informally or not at all. Yet it is in just these up-front reviews that the most important decisions are made about the cost of the development project, the cost of the product, and its strategic and product line fit.

> It is in up-front reviews that the most important decisions determining the cost of the development project, the cost of the product, and its strategic and product line fit are determined.

Product development management is accountable for the entire process: business policy, market research, product mix, product planning, design, production, distribution, and after-sales service. The responsibility for the development of the product has not been separated, as in the case of NEC's laptops, between technical and commercial issues. This is why Fuji Xerox puts a special emphasis on gate reviews to control the flow of over 100 concurrent product development projects.

Review points and review content are established in a charter at the time the product development initiation proposal is prepared. The proposal follows a 40-page fixed format with detailed content and identifies the phase gate and review at which each designated aspect of the proposal will be validated. While Fuji Xerox retains a relatively strong functional organization of its product development activities, senior representatives for each function make up the core team. They report to the general managers of their functions, who together retain ultimate responsibility for quality, cost, and delivery. The program team leader is full time on all of the larger projects, as are the members of the core team. On smaller projects, several may be grouped under a single team leader.

While these examples paint a broad picture of the role that reviews play in the product development process, best practice is in the rigor applied by teams in meeting the criteria specified at each review. These criteria, if met, should help overcome the problems categorized in Chapter Three. Of these, one deserves special attention: customer needs. The question is not only whether the voice of the customer is represented at critical review points but whether that voice has been correctly captured. This is the subject to which we turn.

Notes

1. K. Uchimaru, S. Okamoto, and B. Kurahara, *TQM for Technical Groups: Total Quality Principles for Product Development* (Portland, Ore.: Productivity Press, 1993).

2. Department of the Navy, *Best Practices: How to Avoid Surprises in the World's Most Complicated Technical Process*, NAVSO p-6071 (Washington, D.C.: U.S. Government Printing Office, 1986).

Chapter 9
Product Definition

What happens when someone actually produces all of the same benefits offered by a Mercedes, let's say, but does it optimally? This means offering nothing more and nothing less than what the customer desires, and at a competitive price. That is exactly what Toyota did with the Lexus. It is as good as a Mercedes in the same performance category—some might say better—and it costs a lot less.

The trick, if one can call it that, is to determine in advance exactly what is desired, especially if the development cycle is fast and there is little room for error—in other words, capture the voice of the customer early and definitively. Toyota does just that as a means of defining a new-car specification and even goes to the extent of having individuals live with families to probe their habits and tastes.[1] But many companies do not know exactly what its customers want, even though their skilled marketers and engineers will say they do. If GM knew, it would not produce cars with two keys, one to open the front door and one to start the ignition. If Mercedes really knew, it would produce a car that is as price and market competitive as the Lexus, and it would be a lot richer for it. Toyota, on the other hand, is so rich, reports *Fortune* magazine, that with its current cash reserves it could buy Ford outright.

If disciplined product definition is the goal, capturing the voice of the customer is a key activity. Two traits run through the best practices involved in discovering what the customer is saying and thus lowering the risk of low marketing acceptance. First is sampling small numbers of customers—no more than 20 to 25, especially if they are lead users, or customers with a propensity to try new things. Lead users provide immediate feedback on the benefits or value new ideas might bring to them.

Second, all members of a development team must have direct contact with the customers for whom they are designing a product. This is instrumental in meeting the driving principle of delivering the whole business's capabilities in the service of the customer. Traditional arm's-length surveys or focus group techniques can be used as well, but those are generally most useful in confirming whether needs are being met.

Product Definition

Product definition at Hewlett-Packard is treated as the transition between a well-defined strategy and the actual conceptualization of a design. It is an intensive information-gathering stage aimed at covering as many bases as possible with documented answers.

Edith Wilson, a manager on the corporate staff, set out in 1990 to determine why certain projects failed and others succeeded.[2] In 66 percent of the failures she analyzed, *user needs understanding* was acknowledged as weak. Among these failed projects, 50 percent of them lacked strategic alignment or charter consistency; another 50 percent of the failures did not carry out a *competitive analysis*. And 33 percent had not studied *regulatory compliance* requirements or *product channel* issues.

As a result of her study, Wilson developed a list of 12 critical factors:

1. Establishing strategic alignment
2. Investigating regulatory issues
3. Identifying user needs
4. Carrying out a competitive analysis
5. Planning product positioning
6. Establishing project priorities
7. Determining links to R&D technology
8. Determining manufacturing technologies
9. Determining marketing techniques
10. Calculating the project's strategic dependencies
11. Determining project leadership
12. Anticipating resource needs

Miss any one on the sequence and you will most likely run into trouble later, she proposed. "In many cases," related Wilson,

> a team is tempted to jump into a project and start spending resources on an idea without even checking on whether it is aligned with the strategy of the firm. This invariably leads to problems that mean stopping and restarting. This happens, too, when engineers take a technology and start running without bothering to study user needs or competitors.

On the list, one item stood out as most problematic: *inadequate analysis of user needs.*

If the product definition is to be robust, advises Wilson, each one of these 12 factors has to be accounted for prior to funding authorization and execution of the project. On one project, 28 team members rated the critical factors on a scale of 1 to 5:

	Mean	*Standard Deviation*
1. Strategic alignment	3.7	0.9
2. Regulatory issues	3.8	1.0
3. User needs understanding	2.8	0.9
4. Competitive analysis	2.9	1.5
5. Product positioning	2.8	0.7
6. Project priorities	—	—
7–9. Technical risk	4.3	—
10. Strategic dependencies	4.2	0.7
11. Leadership	—	—
12. Resources	4.3	—

The team rated itself as weak in three areas (items 3, 4, and 5), and there was a wide dispersion of views on item 4. Equipped with this simple ranking, they could now tackle these problem areas before moving on. Not to would add enormous risk of failure to the project. "Strengthening the product definition through a studied attention to each of these twelve factors," points out Wilson, "creates real value to HP's business."[3] In addition to communication among team members, it leads teams to identify common goals, highlight risks, and helps avoid the ultimate nemesis of product development efforts, or what Wilson terms "creeping featurism" (the irresistible temptation by engineers or marketers to add just one more feature). This is always easier the less one knows about what a customer actually wants.

Quality Function Deployment

One of the most original techniques for product definition surfaced in the Japanese shipyards during the late 1960s. A professor, Yoji Akao, developed a method for cascading specific customer requirements into and throughout the design, production, and delivery stages of a ship. He perfected a system of matrices (quality tables) linking the requirements of one step to the solutions built into the next. Akao called it *quality function deployment* (QFD), meaning the deployment of customer requirements into each subsequent development step. As he put it:

> Quality function deployment provides specific methods for ensuring quality throughout each stage of the product development process, starting with design. In other words, this is a method for developing a design quality aimed at satisfying the customer and then translating the consumers' demands into design targets and major quality assurance points to be used throughout the production stage.

To assure the quality of new products, we must pay close attention not only to the 'negative quality' perception expressed in consumer complaints but also to the unspoken or latent 'positive quality' ideas expressed in consumer demands.

> To assure the quality of new products, we must pay close attention not only to the "negative quality" perception expressed in consumer complaints, but also to the unspoken or latent "positive quality" ideas expressed in consumer de-

mands. . . . With new products we must begin by learning
what to assure.[4]

In short, a technique was needed to distinguish types of needs
and to prioritize what one would ultimately offer the customer.

QFD evolved rapidly as a methodology that requires the
full involvement of a product development team from the start
in gathering voice-of-the-customer (VOC) requirements and defining product concepts and designs based on them. It meant a
sustained effort to keep the VOC actively involved throughout
the development cycle, with formal reviews to ensure that VOC
needs were constantly fed back into the development process.

QFD is cumbersome to carry out and thus not for everyone.
Its greatest merit is that it engages a full development team in
gathering a wide span of information and discussing together
how best to structure it into a total picture of their project. This
type of discussion reveals gaps in knowledge, skills, resources,
and competitive intelligence that can be caught early in the
product definition process. In this manner key items, such as
technological engineering bottlenecks, can be isolated for special
effort and attention.

The basic QFD tool is a quality table or matrix that arrays a
decomposition of requirements on the vertical side and design
solutions for each requirement on the horizontal side (Exhibit 9-
1). Where each intersects, a high, medium, low, or no correlation
is noted. Each of the horizontal requirement columns can be extended to the right side to include customer ratings of competitive products and how they meet each requirement. These data
are used to strategize which requirements to focus on in order to
differentiate the product from those of competitors. The vertical
design solution rows can be extended at the bottom to show the
degree of technical difficulty involved in meeting it, an effective
way of judging whether technology should be developed in-
house or purchased externally. The quality table thus displays
all information required to define the product or service that
will be produced and delivered to the market.

> The quality table displays all information required
> to define the product or service that will be pro-
> duced and delivered to the market.

Poorly executed QFD and quality tables lead to an incomprehensible morass of information and unhappy employees, one reason why so many Western companies have turned away from it in despair. It is best learned not as a classroom technique but by applying it to an actual project, with professional facilitation.

Of NEC-NIMS's first experiences with QFD in 1984, its president, Kiyoshi Uchimaru wrote: "[We] set up research teams that eventually generated a massive quality table, two meters by two meters [or about six feet by six feet]. These voluminous tables were too large to be of any practical use. Moreover, they were too complex and took far too much time to produce for each product. The reason they were so large was that we made them without carefully planning their purposes, and followed the textbook blindly." Within two years, the company had learned to downsize the matrices to a manageable size. "These new quality tables were of great value," he wrote, "to those in direct charge of engineers because they clearly explained the concept and flow of each design plan."[5]

Juki is the world's leading industrial sewing machine company. Headquartered not far from Tokyo, its CEO, an ex-Imperial Navyman, uses World War II imagery to build a nationalistic fervor to compete. Winning is the corporate mission. And this is exactly what the firm set out to do when it saw an opportunity in the mid-1980s to reach into unfamiliar waters, the home market for electronic sewing machines. A disciplined quality-driven company, Juki decided to make QFD a principal technique for mastering the design of a sewing machine.

Several years later, one of us saw the product of that effort: a well-worn document that was unfolded into a truly gigantic quality table counting hundreds of items, minutely and laboriously entered by hand on each of the vertical and horizontal axes. To the untrained eye, it was incomprehensible, not to mention illegible. This exercise, completed by the development team, had led to the introduction of a fully electronic home sewing machine—and to a jarring outcome: a total and expensive flop. It had so many features that no one could be trained to use it, so no one bought it.

Undeterred, Juki labored on and in the process learned some important lessons. "We will never do so detailed a matrix again," said the project manager, with a hidden sigh of relief, "but," he was quick to add, "we learned so much doing it that could be used in the next round of design." They went back to the original customer requirements and diligently prioritized preferred features. In so doing, they discovered potential niche markets in which a grouping of customized features could generate special sales. When the next machine came off the production line, it was leaner, less feature laden, cheaper to build, and priced competitively. QFD tables were still alive and well. "We only use them now to solve very specific problems," offered the team leader as he displayed matrices with only 30 or so items on each axis.

> The greatest benefit is communication between the software engineer and the user. The QFD *process* is better than its output, the quality tables.

In general, Japanese companies have learned to use the tables selectively and in smaller dimensions so teams can deal with bite-sized problems in a more holistic fashion and reach solutions through more integrative deliberations. One of the more vigorous proponents of this approach is Yoshiaki Katayama, president of Japan Systems Corporation (JSC), a large systems software house. An author of many articles on QFD, Katayama is very pragmatic in his judgment of QFD. Hard, measurable benefits are difficult to establish in his view. "The greatest benefit is communication between the software engineer and the user," he feels. "This gives the engineer much better control over changes when and if they happen." He concludes "that the QFD *process* is better than its output, the quality tables. What is best is that is converts chaos into orderly expressions." In his company, Katayama never insists that a team use QFD. "They can do it only if they think it will help them."

QFD migrated to the United States starting with Ford Motor in 1984 and its introduction by Don Clausing of MIT. Since then, several hundred tables have been created at Ford, and a software application developed to facilitate their construction and manipulation. Ford stresses the "QFD is a *planning* tool that identifies the significant items on which to focus time, product improvement efforts and other resources." The development of software tools, such as the one Ford created, or others such as QFD Capture developed by ITI, an Ohio-based firm, or Rockwell International's own QFD software developed for internal use, is uniquely American. Certainly it is doubtful whether any American team could sustain an interest in QFD without a software tool to support drafting of tables. Surprisingly, no equivalent commercial software packages exist in Japan.

Of the many Western companies now applying QFD, Digital is among the more prolific users. It was exposed to the methodology when an employee, Lou Cohen, took a training course from a local organization in February 1986. The first pass at applying QFD to a transaction processing software project, says Cohen "was like the blind leading the blind." It took too long without any closure and the market segment was not well defined. "If we did not do it better," he recalls, "it was going to go nowhere fast." The next trial was with a high-performance-system quality group. The team was small, steps were outlined, and appropriate amounts of time allocated. Customer inputs were used to drive the process, and the team intentionally kept the quality table to a manageable proportion. From this effort, the team agreed, a clear sense of direction was achieved. These experiences confirmed Katayama's conclusion that QFD is not to be judged as a tool but as a communication process for development team members.

With this experience to build on, Digital managers tried a third time, this time on a major project, the VAX 9000. The team, consisting of 15 senior managers, used the method to arrive at a common vision of the project and were able to accept key trade-offs early on—something rarely done early and usually fought over at far greater cost later in the process. This experience launched QFD as a recommended practice and has since been applied in hundreds of situations, mostly unmonitored or untracked by any single group within the company. Cohen's early experiences led him to devise an innovative 2- to 3-day process.

"By doing it fast," he suggests, "you get 80 percent of the benefit and none of the resistance to building complex and unwieldy tables. Prework is the key. It means that people come prepared."

Cohen recommends gathering the voice of the customer through a variety of means, including contextual inquiry. He also recommends prework in carefully planning the pace of the QFD exercise by a team. This means clearly defining key customers, preparing the two-day schedule logistics, and carefully selecting the participants.

Day 1, he advises, is best spent building an affinity diagram, or logical groupings, of well-gathered VOC requirements and then rank-ordering these groupings using a mathematical weighting system. The afternoon is spent doing affinity diagrams of product features. Participants list key ideas and order them into logical groupings, which can then be prioritized in importance.

Day 2 is spent correlating requirements and features. Product features are prioritized and a follow-up action plan established.

This quick and dirty application of the methodology "works well as a team building tool," says Cohen. "And it forces us right away to start asking the embarrassing questions. Do we really know what we are doing?" Significantly, too, it motivates design engineers to meet customers face to face in order to understand their needs.

AT&T's experiences diverge significantly from Digital's even though it was Lou Cohen who introduced AT&T to QFD techniques in 1987 during an exchange of ideas between companies. Four years later, AT&T counted 30 successful applications with increased use in service, planning, and process improvement. Susan Brown, a technical staff member at Bell Laboratories, coordinated a seven-person group that used QFD to develop a two- to five-year plan for a 50-person software technology department (STD). They asked internal customers what should be in the plan, mapped those requirements into eight quality tables, and selected one of those tables for more intensive analysis. This effort evolved over a seven-month period, with the team investing 1,100 person-hours during 200 hours of working together. Was it worth the effort? "Absolutely," says Brown.

"The STD gained a far better understanding of its products, processes, and shortfalls. We did learn important lessons. Interviewing training would be worthwhile as is some basic QFD training for the team and with a very well trained facilitator to support it."

Although QFD was first used as a way of building customer requirements into the design and production of hardware products, it has migrated into other product areas such as software and services. Procter & Gamble has used QFD to redesign its relationship with distributors and government regulatory agencies. Hans Hjort, president of Innovata and a QFD consultant, uses QFD to assist firms in developing long-term strategies. In addition, he used quality tables to help Volvo conceptualize an electric prototype car for demonstration at a high-profile auto show. He makes effective use of star diagrams to contrast planned and competitive product features as rated by a QFD analysis. "These star diagrams offer a team an instantaneous picture of strengths and weaknesses in their products measured against competitors'," he says. "They can much more easily strategize positioning of a product based on these diagrams."

The overriding benefit of QFD is that it stimulates communication between members of a team and their customers. Since failed communication is one of the biggest obstacles to high performance in large corporations, QFD is, in our view, a best-practice approach to overcoming those hurdles.

Translating the Voice of the Customer Into Products

Because so many companies have taken the customer's voice for granted, almost anything they do in this area will be an improvement. The intent is to gather unfiltered, first-hand commentary from users of a product or service. But because these comments are always expressed in terminology or language unique to the user, they need to be translated. That translation into a company's own technical language allows solutions to be brainstormed, with greater likelihood of arriving at one that most effectively meets the needs expressed.

Concept engineering, one of the VOC best practices to

emerge in the 1990s, is a collage of methods synthesized by the Center for Quality Management in Cambridge, Massachusetts, a consortium of companies. The center developed a 15-step VOC procedure, termed *concept engineering*, that leads to a carefully crafted breakdown of requirements and a methodology for quantifying each requirement so that a design team can conceptualize a coherent solution:

Understanding the customer's environment
1. Plan for exploration.
2. Collect the voice of the customer.
3. Develop a common image of environment.

Converting understanding into requirements
4. Transform the voice of the customer into requirements.
5. Select significant requirements.
6. Develop insight into requirements.

Operationalizing what has been learned
7. Develop and administer questionnaires.
8. Generate metrics for requirements.
9. Integrate understanding.

Concept generation
10. Decompose.
11. Generate ideas.
12. Generate solutions.

Concept selection
13. Screen solutions.
14. Select concepts.
15. Reselect and finalize.

The procedure, which can take 6 to 12 weeks for a team to complete, produces all the information needed to fill in the vertical axis of a quality table. The process ensures that a true representation of the voice of the customer is merged into the product development process.[6]

Several well-developed techniques were combined into the 15-step procedure:

- *Customer interviewing* techniques used by teams in the field
- *Contextual inquiry* methods of gathering customer ideas by observing them in their own environment
- *Affinity diagrams* (also called the *KJ method*) allow teams to build idea maps quickly and effectively
- *Tree diagrams,* which formalize total quality management techniques for decomposing general ideas into more and more specific ones
- The *Kano method,* which leads to the discovery of latent needs and the specification of user requirements

Bose, a CQM member company, decided to apply concept engineering because "we found that fully half our development weaknesses were definition and specification related. We didn't have correct or complete data at the beginning of a given project, so we learned too late that our specifications did not define the requirements of the customer's intended use of the product." Despite strong resistance, management pushed a product team to apply concept engineering. "Stubborn as we were, our attitude began to change through the interviewing process. We heard comments on issues we'd never addressed before, and we learned that some of our assumptions had been faulty. If we hadn't heard it with our own ears, we never would have believed some of what we learned."[7] Exhibit 9-1 shows the findings developed from the team's direct interviewing of customers.

> Stubborn as we were, our attitude began to change through the interviewing process. We heard comments on issues we'd never addressed before, and we learned that some of our assumptions had been faulty. If we hadn't heard it with our own ears, we never would have believed some of what we learned.

VOC research became a business byword in the early 1990s. Some of the results hit the car industry in 1995 at the annual

Exhibit 9-1. Bose image—KJ method.

What Scenes or Images Come to Mind When You Visualize Ceiling Mounted Speakers?

Customers Prefer a High Quality Sound Experience.

Bose Commercial Products Are Hard To Sell

Winning bids are submitted with hidden costs

CTNs of Xfmrs. spkrs and grills being assembled by min. wage worker

Quick and Dirty contractor fabs support - install kits from scrap studs

Bose designs have impediments to easy sale

Salesman curses "That Damned Controller!"

Even if you tell them it's flame retardant plastic, it's a big fight so we just go with the metal grill.

We like Bose, but your Price Point is too High

A lot of people want the good sound but they get sticker shock when they look at the price.

He wants something more than the basic speaker. The 102 is a Rolls Royce. He needs Cadillac.

Good sound can influence the choices that customers make.

Result of our demo: we won over Altek 419C

They come from Chicago to Madison for the sound at Roller Rink.

I want a hifi experience at my business.

It has to sound like you're at home.

I want a small package that kicks.

You can do a small intimate restaurant where the guy is a music buff and you put in 8 speakers which is more than the room dictates but he wants seamless coverage.

People are increasingly dissatisfied with the limitations of poor quality speakers.

We're typically the 3rd or 4th system in. The others didn't work, you couldn't understand the voice.

We're delivering CD quality music into telephone quality speakers.

Nothing is worse than listening to a crappy speaker played loud.

Installers Are Forced to Improvise During Installation.

I have to put a guy-wire to the ceiling on every speaker because of the L.A. Earthquake spec.

Installers are indignant towards installation hardware shortcomings.

The WB 16 brackets: whoever invented those needs to be beaten with them.

It's a real bummer if you're on the job site and you don't have everything.

Paint darkens when it hits a cloth grill. It's a pain in the ass for a painter to make a 2nd lighter batch.

I stack three tiles over a bucket and cut with a hole saw.

Once Installed the Customer Doesn't Want to Think About It Again.

Speakers should be heard and not seen.

The trend is going invisible, or pretty close to invisible.

Customer during a retrofit: "Don't replace my grill."

People want a speaker that matches the drop down light environment, and other architectural environments.

I like tamper-proof equipment because "Everyone thinks they're a DJ."

Source: "Bose Enchilada Project," *CQM Journal* 3, no. 2 (1994): 47. Used by permission of Bose.

North American International Auto Show in Detroit. This was the year of "surprises and delighters," one journalist reported in a newspaper article entitled "Detroit's Cup Holders Runneth Over." Cup holders, a decade-old phenomenon, were the head-lining news item in a new crop of cars. Yet even the best cus-tomer research on the need for cup holders can end up in the most counterproductive form. The same journalist elected GM the "cup holder champion with a whopping 14 in each of its mini-vans. Mini-vans generally carry up to seven passengers." But, he added, "since most of the holders can be used only when the van's rear seats are folded down, the number of usable cup holders varies inversely with the number of people with cups."[8]

Getting it right is a lengthy affair, and each of the 15 concept engineering steps involves different combinations of techniques and tools. Two of these, *customer interviewing methods* and *contex-tual inquiry*, are explained below. GM's cup-holding minivan ap-pears to have done the first well but ignored the second.

Customer Interviewing

Capturing the voice of the customer is not something reserved to marketers or salespeople. It is something everyone on a devel-opment team does. Edward McQuarrie is a widely respected guru of customer interviewing methods as well as an academic at the University of Santa Clara in California.[9] A sense of humor serves him well in bringing something as arcane as "how to in-terview a customer" to life in front of a generally less-than-inter-ested audience of product development engineers. Engineers are not always gregarious; some turn out to be quite shy when it comes to meeting strangers, particularly customers. Many are so wrapped up in their technology that the world is defined through the lens of that technology. This often leads to long dis-courses on what the company is planning next, a direction to a conversation that brings heart palpitations to a salesman who may be closing a sale on a product that might soon be obsoleted. The engineer is likely, too, to tell the customer what he or she needs. Listening is not an engineer's strong card.

Then there are marketers. They usually enter a room full of self-confidence about market trends, what ideas will really hit in the market, and requests for inclusion of last-minute features just as a product nears production. When it comes to knowing the voice of the customer, the marketer knows it and will freely offer personal opinions of what the requirements should be.

These two characterizations are far from exaggerated, and they result in poor communication, a lot of misinformation, and a less-than-adequate understanding of the customers for whom a product or service is being designed. This, of course, is just what Edith Wilson was talking about when she studied why projects succeeded or failed at Hewlett-Packard. At the top of her list was understanding user needs.

| Discovery is what you are looking for. |

McQuarrie recommends planning interviews by having open-ended questions prepared in advance. The open-ended approach provides the interviewee ample room to digress or expand on a topic. This not only yields unexpected dividends but avoids freezing the person into simple yes-no answers. "Discovery is what you are looking for," says McQuarrie. "Mass mailings of surveys don't lead to discovery." This often grates at the marketing people who thrive on sending out long lists of questions and then compiling seemingly hard data out of the responses. The so-called hard data generally confirm only what is already known about a particular group of customers. It fails in exploring new avenues of ideas or thoughts.

McQuarrie advocates sending two individuals to the interview: one to ask the questions in an informal way and the other to take notes. "Always leave time at the end for a question such as, 'Is there anything else you'd like to comment about?' Many times you'll get the most unexpected remarks that way." He suggests, too, that after the interview, the two-person team immediately debrief by recording as exactly as possible the actual customer words used. This taps fresh memories and clarifies any ambiguities in the interview. "What surfaced as truly significant," says Richard Paynting, chief engineer at Bose, "was that it led to understanding the motivation underlying a customer's expression of a requirement. This was new to us. It led to discovering some significant latent needs."

| What is most important is that the team members develop a deep and shared understanding of user needs. |

Invariably, the team members return enlightened and invigorated by having direct contact with customers or distributors, and equipped with insights that are both new to the team and unexpected. Most important, the team members develop a deep and shared understanding of user needs so they can more quickly create sketches of ideas and carry them back to the customer as a catalyst for further refinements.

Contextual Inquiry

Similar results come from another VOC research method, contextual inquiry.[10] The team identifies key clients—generally ones who are willing to risk buying new products—who are termed lead users or early adopters, and spends an extended amount of time observing how they work and the role a particular product plays in that work environment. "This gives us a far better vision of the system," says Yogesh Parikh of Digital, "by seeing the working links between an individual, his group, and his organization." A clear picture of work structures, work concepts, work intentions, and work outputs is gained, which "can then be tied to a system structure, system concepts, functionality, and system artifacts."

The shortcomings of many conventional research techniques helped fuel the development of contextual inquiry methods. Telephone interviews provide no context and limited responses; formal questionnaires yield little or no design data; traditional interviews fall short in generating design data and small sample sizes; focus groups allow one or two people to dominate and reveal little or no design data; and laboratory studies have uncertain carry-over to real-life contexts and few real motivation or time constraints.

In contrast, a well-executed contextual inquiry yields information about experiences as they occur in the client's workplace. From such observations come insights that otherwise might never surface. When disposable diapers were first marketed in Japan, U.S. companies sold and distributed them in large boxes. Their sales were meager at the same time that Japanese diapers were stealing market share. Contextual inquiry might have revealed both the diminutive size of retail stores and the limited storage space in Japanese households. There just was no room to display or store the American-sized boxes.

What is recorded is also analyzed during the interview and observation. Using affinity diagrams, the team will analyze all the findings and synthesize them into a shared vision or focus of the system and the design ideas that might naturally emerge. From this knowledge, says Yogesh Parikh, a paper prototype design can be developed that is "fast, no waste of effort, easily changeable." This can generate rapid feedback from customers and be reiterated by design engineers. By the end of the cycle, the team arrives at a "concrete, integrated system vision."

At Kimberly-Clark Service and Industrial operations in the United Kingdom, similar concerns led a study team to conclude that "current research was delivering its objectives, but was rigid, focused, and distanced from the customer." Because the company had not expanded its breadth of interactions with its customers, said the report, "we didn't know what products were actually used for." This insight led the company to restructure its methods of gathering critical information. One of its innovations was the creation of a "customer watching" methodology.[11] This meant taking teams into the field and observing the environment in which their products were used. An 11-step procedure was recommended:

1. Make the end user comfortable with your presence.
2. Position yourself where verifiable events will be visible.
3. Wait for the event to happen.
4. Note what happens when the event occurs.
5. Wait for events to repeat.
6. Note differences between events.
7. After two or more events, ask the end user about topic guide issues.
8. Take photographs, with the end user's agreement (optional).

9. Ask the end user to narrate the past in relation to the event.
10. Ask the end user to comment on your definition of need.
11. Thank the end user for his or her help.

Customer watching initially was carried out by a senior product developer who spent two days at a variety of sites observing his company's "disposal wipes" products in actual use at a gas station. He watched those who installed, serviced, and used the product to determine why they did not dispense towels as well as they should: "The reason for the problem became clear. In petrol [gas] stations the product was installed on a circular pole enabling the user to access it from virtually all angles. In other installations it was attached to a wall and hence accessible only from one side, as intended." From these and other insights, the development team accumulated 20 important opportunities for improvement to the design of their product.[12]

Latent Needs

Noriako Kano and his colleagues at Tokyo Rika University came up with a new way of classifying VOC statements. Behind their work was a realization that most users of products and services have needs that are invisible to them. No one knew, for example, that they needed Walkman or Macintosh computers with hypercard stacks in them. Probing further, Kano concluded that three kinds of needs can be discovered. One he labeled *must be's*. These are things that must exist for a person even to consider buying a product. In a car, for example, the starter must start the car. This is a "must be." Another category he labeled *one-dimensional*. Gas mileage is an example. A customer is more or less satisfied depending on the mileage but will not turn away because it doesn't meet an explicit value. Finally, Kano distinguished a third and more elusive category, called *attractive features* or what some have termed *delighters*. These are characteristics such as a car radio that automatically tones down when the ringing telephone is lifted off the receiver. Having this feature delights. Not having it is not noticed. Often delighters become "must be's." These categories, mapped out on two axes into what is known as a Kano diagram, show three curves displaying the ranges of customer preference (Exhibit 9-2).[13]

To arrive at these distinctions, Kano developed a clever questionnaire methodology that takes a single question and asks it first in the positive: "If you had [a particular item] how would you feel?" and then in the negative: "If you did not have [this item] how would you feel?" Five similar answers are offered to each question. By making correlations between answers, Kano determines whether the user thinks of the question topic as a must be, as one-dimensional, or as attractive.

Emerging VOC Practices

As more and more companies develop expertise in capturing the voice of the customer, the state of the art continues to move. It is no longer enough simply to ask the customer what he or she wants. In some industries, such as consumer products, it is

Exhibit 9-2. A Kano diagram.

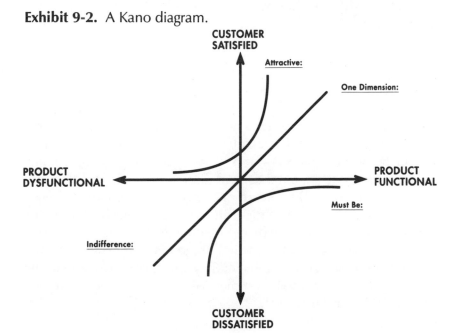

important to look deeply into the beliefs of potential customers. Gerald Zaltman, at the Harvard Business School, invented the Zaltman metaphor elicitation technique that uses images to probe individual belief. "With a very small sample, eight to ten people, I can build a map that explains a comprehensive set of beliefs about a given topic." An example might be "financial success." Individuals are asked to bring several photographs that express their beliefs about the subject. The beliefs are then grouped into headings, such as "living spaces" or "family," or "continuing education." Out of them can be extracted ideas and beliefs that interconnect into a map. These can become the basis for conceptualizing new market or product ideas.

If this sounds fanciful, consider the "Swatchmobile." An 8-foot-long car being produced by the Ste. Suisse Microélectronique et d'Horlogerie, the maker of the Swatch watches, and Mercedes. "We want to make a breakthrough into an additional dimension of traffic," said Helmut Werner, the Mercedes chairman. With the new car, Mercedes wants to combine ecology, emotion, and intellect."[14] These are clearly new marketing appeals and definitely a case of a manufacturer's probing to discover customer wants.

Conclusion

A common thread runs through all of the best practices that have been outlined in this chapter: unfettered lines of communication between customers and developers of products, small sample sizes, and an emphasis on discovery of ideas that might otherwise go unspoken or remain invisible even to the user. Each of the practices is single-minded in pushing for teamwide communication and more disciplined techniques for structuring the concepts, ideas, and data that are generated. The best communication methods are holistic; they call for intensive team interaction and a continual awareness of the entire product system in which they are involved.

Notes

1. This practice got the company in trouble in California when it was discovered that "students" from Japan living with host families were actually Toyota employees looking for consumer data.

2. Edith Wilson Presentation to the IAPD, June 1993.

3. Ibid.

4. Yoji Akao, ed., *Integrating Customer Requirements into Product Design* (Cambridge, MA: Productivity Press, 1988). See also Hans Hjort, ed., *Customer Focused Product Planning and Implementation: Applying QFD* (Fairfield, OH: Innovata, 1993).

5. K. Uchimaru, S. Okamoto, and B. Kurahara, *TQM for Technical Groups* (Portland, OR: Productivity Press, 1993), pp. 56–57.

6. Shoji Sheba, Alan Graham, and David Walden, *A New American TQM: Four Practical Revolutions in Management* (Cambridge, MA: Productivity Press, 1993).

7. Erik Anderson and Jim Sanchez, "Applications of Concept Engineering on the Bose Enchilada Project," *CQM Journal* 3, no. 2 (1994): 42–51.

8. James Bennet, "Detroit's Cup Holders Runneth Over," *New York Times*, January 9, 1995, p. D5.

9. Edward McQuarrie, *Customer Visits* (Newbury Park, CA: Sage, 1993).

10. Yogesh Parikh, "Contextual Inquiry" (presentation to the IAPD, March 1993).

11. From a presentation to the Welsh Development Agency's Time to Market program (1995).

12. Strategem Limited, "A Case Study: Kimberly Clark" (prepared for Time to Market sponsored by the Welsh Development Agency, 1994).

13. The best source for the Kano method is the Center for Quality Management, Cambridge, MA.

14. "Off the Wrist, onto the Road: A Swatch on Wheels," *New York Times*, March 5, 1994.

Chapter 10
Technology Management

Surely what distinguishes the innovative firm from the less innovative is not just that it is more efficient in applying technology in support of its business strategy, but that its business strategy itself is conducive to recognizing, seizing upon, and exploiting technology. . . . The most striking feature of the failure of U.S. firms to compete effectively in high-tech industries is that many of those firms possessed superior technological capabilities.

—Joseph Morone, *Dean, School of Management, Rensselaer Polytechnic Institute,* Winning in High-Tech Markets: The Role of General Management (1994)

Our intention in this chapter is not to make a black-or-white case for or against either Japanese or Western methods of technology management.[1] However, it is important to recognize the basic differences between them and to understand that these differences are directly related to their different outputs: one richer in basic knowledge and science-driven discovery, the other richer in incubating and developing marketable products. For the United States, unfortunately, the largely DOD-fueled basic science agenda is under fire and shrinking in scale. As the *Wall Street Journal* asked on May 22, 1995 "Corporate Research: How

Much Is Worth It? Top Labs Shift Research Goals to Fast Pay-offs." Major companies registered a 20 to 25 percent drop in total R&D spending between 1990 and 1995. At AT&T, for example, the budget declined from a high of $3.3 billion in 1991 to about $2.75 billion at the end of 1994.

James Brian Quinn, of Dartmouth's Amos Tuck School of Business, commented on research planning at AT&T's Bell laboratories: "The heart of research planning was 'to recruit top-flight scientists and let them think up something to do.' Management's task was to select problem areas where knowledge would expand most rapidly." And he quotes Bela Juenz, a world expert on optical information, on the culture he discovered at the labs: "Here the idea is that distances [between offices] are so constructed that you can, if you have an idea, rush over to someone who is an expert, say, on stochastic processes or invented [some exotic] electronic device and consult him. It's so nearby that it takes less time to go over and see an expert than to suppress the idea [as you would in a university setting]."[2] This approach reflects a Western predilection to let the scientist search for surprises in unexpected places; the Japanese predilection is to establish a degree of control that precludes surprises. Given that more and more Western firms are growing increasingly risk averse when it comes to research and development (R&D), the Japanese model of technology management may offer some important best-practice insights. To be sure, their practices are not flawless, as recent and costly setbacks in high-definition television technology have shown, and they are prone to high-stakes battles, as with the high-density compact disc gambit pitting Toshiba against Sony.

A Three-Track R & D Continuum

The typical Japanese R&D continuum follows three separate but interwoven tracks, each market driven and each feeding the next:

1. *Corporate research*, where product development is separated from the immediate technical needs of the operating divisions and focuses on a five- to ten-year horizon.

2. *Group development*, focusing on a three- to five-year horizon.
3. *Business unit development*, aimed at creating specific products, which concentrates on the short-term one- to three-
   year product development process.

But, says Dr. Michiyuki Uenohara, NEC's now retired senior
technology officer, even the differences in each track's time horizon should be left fuzzy in order to create a sense of internal
competition between the tracks. (An illustrative corporate case,
Toshiba, is described in Appendix C.)

| The typical Japanese research and development
| continuum follows three separate development
| tracks, each market driven and each feeding the
| next.

Each of these three tracks maintains direct contact with customers and often does its own market research. The corporate
research track develops new technologies, sometimes demonstrated as "technology parcels." These establish a set of features
that can be tested and evaluated by possible customers. Posi-
tively appraised technology parcels are transferred to a product
group track to be developed into working prototypes. There
may be several alternative prototypes with different sets of features, which will be tested and evaluated by potential customers. This step validates the utility and helps to establish the
robustness of the technology. This iterative evaluation by the
customer is continued as the prototypes are passed to the business units' product development teams. Because of the extensive
earlier customer evaluation, customer requirements can be more
expeditiously fixed at a very early stage in this, the third track
of the R&D continuum. And if a fast idea to production cycle
time is the goal, now measured in 3 to 9 months for many electronics products, an early and definitive requirements freeze is
the single most important facilitator in moving quickly to production.

| If a fast cycle time is the goal, an early and definitive requirements freeze is the single most important facilitator in moving quickly to production.

As described earlier, NEC's laptop facility in Yonazawa has an unequaled record in the speed with which it gets new products to market. For example, in 1992 and 1993, faced with severe pressure from Toshiba and no product to match, NEC saw a quick erosion of its laptop market share. In response, the division fast-tracked a new product from idea to production in 90 days.

Since the sharp dichotomy between customer-driven and science- or knowledge-driven R&D has not existed in Japan to the extent it does in the United States, all three R&D tracks are aimed at the common objective of meeting market needs. Each track views the same, though evolving, needs of the customer from a different time perspective. In this way, each track focuses on different generations of technical solutions to customer needs. These overlapping perspectives provide an enormously rich array of commercially viable solutions. While this approach diminishes the possibility of serendipitous discovery more widely associated with large Western corporate R&D laboratories, it does not preclude discovery. Instead, the discovery is more likely to lead to a deeper technical understanding of customer needs.

When Toyota appoints a leader of a new model development team, the leader spends a month living with a U.S. family within the demographic group targeted and an additional month with a European family before beginning the project. In Japan, a product development team leader is likely to have a technical background. The reason is that someone with technical expertise may be better able to perceive a solution to a need the customer has not yet recognized, provided he or she is able to understand the entire context in which the customer will use the product—hence, the effort to probe the customer's day-to-day world directly.

> A person with technical expertise may be better able to perceive a solution to a need the customer has not yet recognized, provided he or she is able to understand the entire context in which the customer will use the product.

Understanding of unspoken (latent) customer needs works only if it is translated into an enabling technology. The technician will translate the customer's real but unrecognized need into a new and never-before-thought-of product feature, such as an automatic volume reduction of the stereo system when the car telephone is picked up. In most cases, the technician is the person best able to identify the need and make this translation or breakthrough with the full and imaginative use of the available technical solutions.

R&D Strategy vs. Business Strategy

When it comes to corporate track funding, the R&D activities of many U.S. corporations are characterized by divisive resource allocation debates. At the heart of this dissension is the method of funding. To pay for corporate R&D, an allocation, or tax on the business operations, is the preferred method. But it often triggers an antagonistic relationship between the business operations that must pay with "no questions asked" and the corporate labs that spend "without interference."

One alternative is contract funding of the corporate labs by the business operations. In Japanese companies 50 percent or more of all corporate track funding is contracted by product group divisions or business units. But the business units can choose to contract internally or externally, which stimulates the corporate track to be highly competitive. At Canon, the corporate R&D lab must verify marketplace requirements for the technology it is being asked to develop before it accepts the contract.

We haven't met a major Japanese company that uses contract funding exclusively. There is always a requirement for funds with a longer payback and with wider application across the corporation than would arise from contracts with a single business group or division. But even contract funding of a minimum of 50 percent of the corporate track laboratory budget produces more directly marketable technologies and opens communication between the corporate labs and the business operations.

> An emphasis on funding by contracting for corporate R&D capabilities ties together the technology priorities of the business unit, group, and corporate tracks.

Contract funding is a best practice that should be carefully explored if high "hit rates" are expected of technology management programs. An emphasis on funding by contracting for corporate R&D capabilities ties together the technology priorities of the business unit, group, and corporate tracks, preempting antagonistic relationships that often dominate in companies where corporate R&D is funded largely by allocation—much like a fixed tax.

Total R&D funding at the electronics companies we studied in Japan amounts to about 10 percent of sales. Ten percent of this, or about 1 percent of sales, is expended on corporate track research. The balance is expended at the group- and business-unit level.

In many large Western companies the high-profile top corporate R&D function is perceived by the business operations and divisions as more closely tied to the priorities of its senior scientists than to profitable business opportunities. Until recent changes were instituted, this was a widely held image of Xerox's Palo Alto Research Park. "Great thinking, but where's the beef?" was a complaint voiced by business groups being taxed to support the laboratory. And at the operating level, R&D budgets of Western companies are frequently tied to short-term financial goals.

Identifying Core Technologies

At the heart of best practices in technology management is the identification and prioritization of core technologies for funding, established through consistent evaluation and rating of technologies across the company's product families. It is here that communication and agreement between the business operation's marketing personnel and the R&D organization must fuse, product line by product line. The importance of cross-boundary communication through strategic processes teams focused on research development is clear.

> Communication and agreement between the business operation's marketing personnel and the R&D organization must fuse, product line by product line. The importance of cross-boundary communication through strategic processes teams focused on research development is clear.

To do this, marketing must contribute a long-term ten-year product line plan. These can be remarkably straightforward. At Sony, three dominant market requirements drove the development of the Walkman and later the Discman: size, weight, and quality. Each can be expressed as a performance gap metric that must be consistently and continuously narrowed in order to remain competitive. Similarly, the long-range product objectives of color television manufacturers have been simple and unswerving for more than two decades: larger, higher-quality pictures, flat displays, trimmer sets, and lower prices. Art Schneiderman's half-life concept, introduced in Chapter 7, is founded on an understanding of the role such long-term performance trend lines can play, particularly when aimed at achieving a theoretical limit.

> With clear long-term definitions of the customer's requirements, product line by product line and by performance gap, translations can be made into the language of the scientists and the product technicians.

With clear, long-term definitions of the customer's requirements, product line by product line and by performance gap, translations can be made into the language of the scientists and the product technicians. For Sony, the technical challenge of size and weight reduction, without sacrificing the quality of the Walkman, translated into more compact integrated circuits; smaller, longer-life batteries; and low-power-consumption motors, recording heads, and transport systems. For color television manufacturers, the technical priorities became brighter primary color light emitters, greater contrast, and flatter display devices.

At NEC, whose corporate mission is the integration of computers and communications, technologies are prioritized by subject area and then as core to the future of the company. The company has 30 core technologies, some of them important to more than one group or division. A coordinator is appointed for each core technology. Though he must understand the technology, he is an operating business executive, not a technologist. Each core technology is also viewed from the perspective of six separate strategic domains (for example, functional materials and devices, semiconductors, and software). The strategic domain coordinators are chosen from the heads of the group R&D laboratories. NEC's dual management matrix brings technologists together with operating executives to achieve cross-functional management of its priority technology programs. The 30 technologies and six domains are matrixed, with those of greatest importance at the top left. This exercise produces 180 links, each defined by priority level, current position, and required position and reviewed annually.

In a similar fashion, Canon identifies and manages 21 technological priorities for the twenty-first century, with six core technologies highlighted each year. They are managed by teams of technical and operating personnel. Canon, like NEC, manages each core technology from the additional perspective of horizontal competency, such as computer engineering technologies, technical support, and services required.

Bottleneck Engineering

Because core technologies research is always aimed at achieving long-term advantages, prioritization methods are very useful in establishing a pattern of medium- and longer-term technology priorities. But what of the short term? In this case, a methodology known as *bottleneck engineering* is commonly used in Japan, designed to find the hurdles between stretch goals while meeting cost and time targets.

Professor Emeritus Osamu Furukawa of Hiroshima University developed the bottleneck engineering concept as a way of establishing quality goals, or what he terms "ambitious quality," that will fully satisfy specific customer needs.[3] In bottleneck engineering, as in product definition, quality tables (QFD) are used to relate multiple dimensions of information. Four dimensions of information are interrelated:

1. *"Ambitious" characteristics.* What is required to meet fully the customer's known and latent needs and to exceed the characteristics of competitive products.
2. *"Possessed" technologies.* Technologies that the company has in place, robust, and ready to use.
3. *Bottleneck items.* Characteristics for which there are no corresponding technologies that are robust and ready to use.
4. *Required technologies.* A listing of technologies in the development pipeline but not yet robust or ready for use by the company and a list of technologies for which future work is planned.

Each item is rated by a time frame for arriving at a solution: short term or intermediate to long term. The information developed in the ensuing matrix is used to distinguish between technologies that can be developed in the course of a normal development cycle and those that must be further studied and developed off-line. These are the bottleneck problems. In this manner, bottleneck engineering can be used to identify and manage technology selection and funding prioritization.

Within the broader context of the three-track, market-driven R&D continuum, the prioritization of technologies and differentiation between bottlenecks of longer- and shorter-term solution provide a first level of priority for the identification of activities for each of the three tracks of R&D: at the corporate,

group, and business unit level. Bottlenecks of shorter-term solution are the priorities of the business unit- or group-level R&D;
core technologies and bottlenecks of longer-term solution will
be resolved at the group level or contracted to corporate R&D
groups.

In addition to the market-driven R&D agendas characteristic of Japan's most product innovative companies, some funds
must be spent on blue sky projects—those with open-ended outcomes—no matter how practical and market driven the company may be. In the cases of the Japanese electronics companies
studied, approximately 1 percent of sales is allocated to corporate track research. Of this, 50 percent or less is for fundamental
research. With such a small pot, it is particularly difficult to establish priorities. Genya Chiba, vice president of Japan Research
and Development Corporation, has contributed his solution to
this question. In his opinion it is critical to keep the older, senior
scientists from dominating this process. He suggests having
younger, more recent graduates establish their own priority lists
and then pick out and discard the fads. In his view, this ad-
dresses the fact that senior scientists, because of their vested in-
terests, lack an objective view of the blue sky opportunity.

Organizational Links

When it comes to technology management, organizational relationships play a strong role in affecting research outcomes. Dr.
Yamanouchi, a former senior R&D executive at Canon, uses the
term *spousal* to characterize best practice in Japan. By this he
means that at each organizational level—corporate, group, and
business unit—the senior business operating officer and the
head of R&D act as equal partners. Toshiba's technology executive system is also an example of the spousal form of organization. Direction is provided by the corporate Technology Strategy
Committee, which reports to the CEO. It is here that technical
and market priorities are unified under a core technologies program. Corporate-track R&D activities are directed by this committee. At the group level, each of Toshiba's business groups is
supported by a laboratory funded by the group and working

on priorities established by the group. However, the laboratory formally reports to the corporate Technology Strategy Committee. At the business unit level, the operations director is again complemented by a technical director strongly linked to the chief engineer at the group level.

> At each organizational level—corporate, group, and business unit—the head of the business's profit and loss results and the head of R&D act as equals.

Driven by market-defined priorities, the Japanese model thrives on close cross-organization communication and a balance between short-term and longer-term technology objectives. With strong market-driven R&D priorities integrated with those of the business organization and with R&D guaranteed its own direct access to the customer in the marketplace, a strong case can be made for the more holistic spousal organization simply in the proverbial fact that two heads are better than one. More to the point is that it better serves the leveraging of scarce R&D resources, people, money, and time.

These examples, drawing primarily from the experiences of the Japanese electronics and auto industries, describe a process of technology management that has succeeded in increasing R&D hit rates. At the same time, they have led to few, if any, true breakthroughs or discoveries of new technologies. The strength is in the high level of market focus; the weakness is in a lack of true science or knowledge-driven discovery. While this distinction may be true, it leaves untouched a competitive advantage. "It is the skills of Japanese companies at creating systematic organizational knowledge that has allowed them again and again to innovate their way out of crisis."[4] This said, it leaves unacknowledged the role that American research universities have played in supplying Japan with a need for science-driven technological ideas—but that is a topic beyond the scope of this book.

Notes

1. See Marco Iansiti for an excellent insight into advanced Western practices to manage R&D. "Real World R&D: Jumping the Product Generation Gap," *Harvard Business Review* (May–June 1993). He describes a "systems focus" coming into many companies and the use of "integration teams"

2. James Brian Quinn, *The Intelligent Enterprise* (New York: Free Press, 1992), p. 276.

3. See K. Uchimaru, *TQM for Technical Groups* (Portland, Ore.: Productivity Press, 1990), pp. 20, 25–26, 56, 67.

4. Ikujiro Nonaka and Hirotaka Takeuchi, *The Knowledge Creating Company* (New York: Oxford University Press, 1995), p. 19.

Chapter 11
Suppliers as Partners

Whirlpool Corp. is cooking up its first gas range without hiring engineers to create the gas burner system; instead, the design work is being done by Eaton Corp., a supplier that already makes gas valves and regulators for other appliance manufacturers. Whirlpool expects to get its new range to market several months sooner this way.

—*Wall Street Journal*, December 12, 1994

The least vertically integrated of the Big Three, Chrysler depends more heavily than other automakers on outside suppliers. It buys 70% of its components, vs. 50% at Ford and 30% at GM. By including suppliers in the platform teams, Chrysler can draw on them for marketing intelligence and for skills it lacks.

—*Fortune*, January 10, 1994

Many world-class manufacturers have learned to involve suppliers early in the product development process. They understand that leveraging the parent firm's competencies with those of specialized suppliers is one of the keys to building competitive advantage and adding to the agility of the enterprise. The Japanese set out early in the 1950s to build supplier networks, and a growing number of Western-style supplier associations are also reaping the benefits. For example, electronics firms in and around Silicon Valley have pioneered a regional supplier agglomeration, and more recently suppliers have formed unique associations in Wales.

Each of these supplier networks exemplifies a different approach to building value-adding networks. In Japan it is described as *vertical aggregation,* in Silicon Valley as *vertical disaggregation,* and in Wales it is evolving into a hybrid. In each case, the network represents a shift away from a big-company preference for vertical integration (producing as much as possible within the wholly owned corporate umbrella) and greater reliance on external sourcing. When it comes to the product development process, supplier networks translate into early involvement by suppliers in design and manufacturing decisions and longer-term and more predictable relationships with the client company.

Supplier networks are a marked contrast to the earlier vertically integrated approach when a few large players dominated markets. Ford's famed Rouge plant was a fully integrated manufacturing process that received Ford-mined iron ore at one end and rolled out cars at the other end. Subcontractors then operated at arm's length through purchasing departments. In many cases their principal role was to make up for spikes in demand that the large parent company could not account for. Few affected the design process. The best of them were good at meeting specifications.

Japan's Innovation: Vertical Aggregation

In mature Japanese industries, such as the automotive industry, each of the major manufacturers has a tiered structure of suppliers. A limited number of first-tier suppliers, in which the vehicle manufacturer owns a strategic equity position, manages a second tier; they in turn manage a third. This structure was initiated by Toyota in 1954 after a serious strike crippled the company and led it to reconsider its supplier ties. That year, reports Peter Hines, a highly regarded analyst of Japanese practices at the Cardiff Business School in Wales, "Toyota agreed to make 80 percent of payments in cash with the other 20 percent in 60- or 90-day payable bills. This was in contrast to the more typical complete payment of subcontractors by 60- to 150-day bills."[1] This was a critical step in treating the needs of the supplier as valued partners. A senior Toyota executive summarized the rationale for building a new structure:

> After the 1960s, we began to rely on our suppliers' ability to design and produce automotive components for us. Today, we just give them basic ideas and specifications of the components we want for a specific car. They then give us professional ideas and turn them into products. Our job is to maintain the strong ability to judge the technical capabilities and proposals and demand corrections if necessary. We can't actually make the components in-house. We make only engines, transmissions and some important components. That is why our suppliers are so important to us. We'll do whatever we can to help them become competitive because it's good for us.[2]

By the early 1990s, Toyota's dependence on suppliers evolved into a structure consisting of about 200 first-tier suppliers, each linked to 20 subcontractors and a cadre of about 900 other direct suppliers of unique goods or services. First-tier subcontractors, in turn, are linked to 6 to 8 second-level subcontractors. This vertically aggregated system totals 30,000 medium-sized to small entities supplying the parent company.

The cascading structure created at Toyota, and later widely emulated at Japan's largest auto and electronics industries, is a stroke of industrial genius. The leanness and smallness of each Toyota entity ensures better managerial control and substantially less bureaucracy at every level. When contrasted to a top-heavy giant such as GM, with an 800,000-employee organizational pyramid and direct purchasing ties to 10,000 or more suppliers, the sheer bureaucratic heaviness of GM's structure is enough to slow any innovative impulse, particularly if coming from a supplier.

Christian Bruck, a Luxembourg student of the Japanese supplier environment, has this to say in an in-depth analysis of the supplier system in Japan: "For Japanese auto makers, the average level of value-added was a mere 16.5% of total manufactured cost with 82% of total outlays at Toyota and Nissan being spent on materials. There is much less work done in a Japanese company. Consequently it is smaller and operations are simpler."[3] Although the aggregate network is large, this is a lesson in "small is best" that, until the 1990s, eluded the "big is best" ideology that kept Western corporations wedded to high levels of vertical integration.

Open communication is the critical success factor in the network's successful day-to-day operations. "In order to maintain this close, organic linkage between core firm and subcontractor, a great deal of communication, coordination, and guidance must take place between parties," observes T. Minato. "This environment requires more and better information and information collection than at any time in the past."[4] This need led Toyota early in the 1960s to invent a new category of cross-functions for the sole purpose of establishing effective and ongoing cross-departmental and supplier communication.

Communication: "Golf Talk" and "Fun Talk"

Various equipment manufacturers and suppliers in Japan invariably explain that intimate and ongoing communication is a basis for strong partnerships. More unusual, at least to Western ears, is mention of "golf talk" and "fun talk." The terms come from a mania for golf and an almost religious dedication to it as an extension of business activity and from a cultural habit of continuing business conversations in after-hours restaurants and drinking clubs. Many senior managers and executives spend Sunday driving long hours to start a round at a prescribed time with friends and guests. Equally lengthy hours are spent eating, drinking, and driving home after the round. The rituals are central to maintaining relationships with suppliers, customers, senior colleagues, and ex-classmates (many of whom are with competing companies).

What is referred to as "golf talk" occurs at a high level, between senior corporate executives and supplier managers who enjoy the privilege of expensive golf club memberships. The CEO of the parent company might pass on tips such as: "We have given thought to such and such." This is taken as a cue to initiate a business proposal or idea by the guest supplier.

The fact that golf talk has taken place between a parent company executive and a senior supplier executive, often the CEOs, is a signal for subordinates to engage in more specific "fun talk," which often takes place after hours over a meal and drinks. This is a time when informality prevails in Japan, and one can share discrete business information without penalty. Ideas are often sketched out on the back of envelopes.

Fun talk is described as informal, off-the-record, exploratory discussions with key suppliers concerning the components and products a parent company thinks it will need in the future. In fun talk, product objectives are discussed, as are such things as the circuits and component characteristics that may aid in achieving these objectives. This level of informal discussion provides important input to the component supplier's advanced development track. Although no purchase commitments are made, it is not uncommon for a supplier to develop a "bread board" example of the component under discussion for further review with the parent company. (Occasionally fun talk is taken too seriously, and a supplier will go into production without a formal commitment.)

Communication stimulated through golf talk and fun talk is critical to the success of the process. It allows clear messages to be transmitted without complex negotiations or contracts, and it helps to propagate important clues about new advances in technology or market needs.

Purposes of Supplier Networks

Working at its best, a networked supplier system spreads risk, delegates to others the complex tasks of administration, reduces investment and overhead, and, most vital, allows the parent company to concentrate on the highest value-added activities and leverage these with the skills of its suppliers.

Close, long-term, interdependent relationships between suppliers and their equipment manufacturing customers can exist without the supplier's being dominant. Out of these relationships were built *kyoryoku kai*, or partner associations, that help unify companies around a central competitive need. This system propagated just-in-time (JIT) methods, statistical process control (SPC), and value engineering and value analysis, always with a common goal of improving quality and reducing cost.

> Supplier networks allow the parent company to delegate to its suppliers portions of its development projects and thus concentrate its own resources on core technologies and higher-value-added activities.

A significant motivation for the high degree of intimacy is that it increases the resources available to the parent firm's development teams. Given that key suppliers have their own areas of competence, they are chosen specifically for their brains. The supplier can identify and correct errors, influence the design of the final product, and take the responsibility for design and development. In such cases, the supplier's contribution to the development project often begins soon after the preconcept phase. The parent company can then delegate to its suppliers portions of its development projects and concentrate its own resources on core technologies and higher value-added activities, giving it more leverage over its internal resources.

Toyota, for example, delegates to its suppliers the responsibility for the design and development of major subsystems of a car. It retains full control over the platform design, while the headlamp design, for example, is the entire responsibility of the supplier, whose only constraint is the contour and aesthetic look and feel of the "skin" on the outside and the connecting points on the inside.

The Silicon Valley Innovation: Vertical Disaggregation

In the United States the relationships between large companies and their suppliers are changing rapidly. We see this in purchasing departments where tactical, short-term decisions traditionally based on competitive bids from a large supplier base are being replaced by longer-term commitments to a more limited group of suppliers whose capabilities extend beyond quality, cost, and delivery. In many cases the relationship is an actual alliance, with buyer and vendor sharing offices.

Many of the innovators were in Silicon Valley. In 1984, Michael Scott, then Apple Computer CFO, discussed his role in bringing the company to life. "Our business," he said, "was designing, educating, and marketing. I thought that Apple should do the least amount of work that it could and should let everyone else grow faster. Let the subcontractors have the problems." For help with board stuffing, Scott relied partly on Hildy Licht who "operated a cottage industry. Parts were delivered to her home and she distributed them to hand-picked assemblers scattered around the neighborhood, tested the finished work, and returned it to Apple in the back of her brown Plymouth station wagon. She was flexible, could make revisions on boards, and offered overnight service." The strategy paid off. James Brian Quinn of Dartmouth's Tuck School calculated that "in 1977, ten [Apple] employees each averaged about $77,000 in sales; in 1981, 2,400 employees each averaged $139,500. By 1990 the ratio had reached $370,000 per employee."[5] That same year, IBM's ratio was $139,000; Digital Equipment's $85,000; and Data General's $81,000.

The dominant Western trend in outsourcing is to base procurement decisions on the long-term objectives of the parent corporation. To qualify, suppliers must have capabilities that extend beyond bread-and-butter quality, cost, and delivery to include technical excellence, proprietary know-how, cost and performance advantages (value), service excellence, and innovative solutions.

Leading companies in Silicon Valley widely practice early supplier involvement in new-product development. The lore there is that loyalties are not based on the company you work for but the technology to which you are committed. The network's glue is the technology that travels in people's heads. Formal company-to-company links, as in the Japanese model, are secondary. This means continuous job hopping, new start-ups, and ever-changing combinations of alliance and supplier links. The objective is to use the specialized engineering and technical strengths of suppliers wherever they reside. Thus, internal resources can be concentrated on value-adding core capabilities and technologies. In the words of Scott McNealy, CEO of Sun Microsystems "the quality of our products is embedded in the quality of the products we purchase." As a result, Sun saves costly overhead it would otherwise have to cover and ensures itself continued access to the best and brightest ideas in the valley. According to another Sun executive: "If we were making a stable set of products, I could make a solid case for vertical integration." However, by relying on external suppliers, Sun introduced four major new-product generations in its first five years of operation, doubling the price-performance ratio in each successive year. Market share responded and quickly boosted the company into the billion-dollar-a-year club.

For Silicon Graphics' Edward McCracken,

> the fact that the semiconductor companies are right nearby is really critical to us, and has been since we started (it's even reflected in our name). Our hardware strategy coincided with the chip companies getting booted out of the commodity business and shifting to serve our needs of increasing miniaturization and specialization. This coincidence of supply and demand created a whole new breed of computer companies.[6]

> One of the things that Silicon Valley lets you do is minimize the cost associated with getting from idea to product. Vendors here can handle everything.

Echoing this strength peculiar to the Valley, Les Denend, an executive at 3Com, stated:

> One of the things that Silicon Valley lets you do is minimize the costs associated with getting from idea to product. Vendors here can handle everything. If you specify something— or, as is often the case, if the vendor helps you specify it—you can get hardware back so fast that your time-to-market is incredibly short. This means that the majority of our vendors are here. Silicon Valley has an incredibly deep ven-

dor base, and it is intensely competitive. You can build relations with vendors here that are not replicable elsewhere.

The phrases *vertical disaggregation* and *regional aggregation*
characterize relationships developed between firms in Silicon
Valley. They are the opposite of vertical integration in that the
firms extend outward within the region to build their capabilities. The extended enterprise, particularly associated with supplier networks or associations, puts even greater emphasis on
effective cross-organization communication for the same reasons that Japanese observers noted. There are more players dealing with more complex solutions and working under tighter
constraints. This redefines the concept of teaming in product
development to include external members as integral participants in the product development process from the start.

The Welsh Hybrid: A Shared Learning Network

Wales may not be the first place many people would think of
looking to for insight into world-class suppliers, yet it is exactly
that. The Welsh Development Agency (WDA) has managed an
aggressive campaign to transform the regional economy from a
coal- and steel-based production culture to a diversified manufacturing base. Much like New England's escaping its textile and
shoe manufacturing past and turning into a high-tech electronics mecca during the 1950s and 1960s, the Welsh transition
has come full circle, a fact punctuated in 1994 by the near closing
of Wales's last officially functioning coal mine. In January 1995,
ownership of the Tower Mine in South Wales, the last working
deep mine, was turned over to its workers. The rest of the mines
have been shut down and the giant slag mountains built up
around them graded, grassed, and turned over to sheep.

These efforts did not go unnoticed by Japanese firms seeking a base of operations within the European economic community; 45 of them are now located in a largely rural area with a
population of only 3 million. Attracted by an available work-
force and generous government subsidies, this influx brought
with it an equal infusion of new managerial practices, stimulat-

ing the birth of a dynamic regional economy that stands out as an exemplar equal to the oft-referenced European "mini-motors": Baden Wurttemberg (Germany), Lyons (France), Barcelona (Spain), Milan (Italy), and Cambridge (England).

In this environment appeared a group of innovators, including Peter Hines, at the Cardiff Business School. A student of Japanese management, in 1991 he saw an opportunity to work with the WDA in building a Welsh-styled supplier association—a Westernized *kyoryoku kai*. He combined forces with two senior WDA staff, Dennis Turner and Paul Morris, a project manager, as well as an external consultant, George Longworth. Since that time 15 supplier associations have come to life and yet others put into planning stages, the first taking root around Calsonic Llanelli Radiators (CLR). Each of these groups counts between 8 and 12 members and in one case as many as 23. An immediate innovation was including direct and indirect (or second-tier) suppliers rather than limiting association membership, as in Japan, to first-tier companies. Their focus, new to all of these companies, is on shared learning and establishing common objectives around the needs of the parent firm.

The most important impact, at least in the first year, is in building intercompany relationships.

CLR has felt the benefits of the network established in early 1992 in the design, costing, and delivery areas and more subjectively in the growth of a new supplier culture. Both direct and indirect supplier firms have been rewarded with increased business as they improved their performance levels. The most important impact, however, at least in the first year, is in building intercompany relationships. As a result, CLR and the supplier association members have jointly developed value engineering and value analysis plans necessary to meet exacting cost and quality targets set by the large car assemblers they supply. Defect levels from member suppliers fell 50 percent in the first year and a further 30 percent in the second year. Stocks were reduced by 34 percent while sales and turnover increased. When it came to new product development, CLR was able to bring products to the market within targeted costs for the first time. From 1990, prior to being purchased by Calsonic and a large infusion of modernization capital, when the company's market share of European automotive car radiators was a slim 2 percent, it jumped to 14 percent by 1994 and is expected to continue rising.

Tom Howie of EET Limited, a supplier to CRL, reflects:

> The supplier association initiative has given EET an opportunity to develop a true partnership with Calsonic, rather than the traditional arms-length customer/supplier relationship. It provides a communication system for timely information on Calsonic's plans and contracts, which enables us to plan future capacity and quality requirements ahead of schedule. The associated development program, with its emphasis on joint continuous improvement . . . and the development of best practices, has benefited EET across the whole of its customer base and has enabled the firm to develop links with other Calsonic groups abroad.

Pleased with the results, the WDA has since branched the shared learning concept outward. In 1992, it funded the establishment of a six-company group to study and apply best practices in product development. Comanaged by the authors of this book, the WDA, and a Manchester-based firm, Strategem, the success of this effort led to the founding of a second best-practice group. As with the supplier associations, the breakthrough has been most visible in the willingness of member companies to share their success and failure experiences with colleagues from other firms.

Supplier Partnerships

Deciding to involve external suppliers as partners early in the product development process is a long-term strategic decision, not a short-term tactical one. Indeed, during the 1970s and 1980s, observers called attention to the "hollowing" of Western industrial strength in industries such as consumer electronics where too many outsourcing decisions were made purely for crisis-induced tactical reasons. In contrast, the involvement of suppliers as partners in product development is a long-term strategy. It requires the parent company to carefully, systematically, and continuously identify and reidentify technologies that are core to its business strategy—not just today but as far into the future as it can see. These core technologies are kept in-house. Others are managed through alliances, strategic partnerships, or joint ventures.

At Bose, in Framingham, Massachusetts, preferred suppliers are invited to establish offices within the company. This encourages direct contact with product development teams and the manufacturing managers. The closeness of the relationship has been extended by Bose to the point of issuing blank purchase orders for the suppliers to fill out as needed, a practice that has accelerated response times and eliminated the need for purchasing staff to process the paperwork.

A partnership is vastly different from the "master-slave" relationships that historically have characterized U.S. original equipment manufacturers and their suppliers. Master-slave has been the predominant pattern in U.S. companies and generally describes how suppliers in Japan treat the smallest companies on the lowest rungs. In the master-slave case, specifications for the entire product and its components and subsystems are developed by the parent company and put out for competitive bid. In partnerships, the supplier contributes to the concept and to the specifications that define the product. It functions as an integral part of the product development team, designing and developing parts and subsystems.

These Japanese, American, and Welsh models are based on a broad realization that the complexity of products and the logistics involved in getting them to market is making it less and less possible for a single corporation to master all the ingredients that go into successful product development. The outcome is a natural and rapid evolution toward networks of competencies. And although any single supplier's unique competence may be available to all competitors in a particular product or service category, the winners are the companies with the managerial skill to deliver the whole in the service of the customer most effectively.

Notes

1. Alex Taylor III, "Will Success Spoil Chrysler?" *Fortune*, January 10, 1994.

2. Peter Hines, quoted in *Creating World Class Suppliers* (Pitman Publishing—Financial Times Series, 1994), p. 129.

3. Christian Bruck, "Japanese Management of Subcontracting" (master's thesis, Keio University, 1988), p. 11.

4. Ibid.

5. The Scott and Quinn quotations are from James Brian Quinn, *Intelligent Enterprise* (New York: Free Press, 1992), pp. 65–66.

6. Ibid., p. 124.

Chapter 12

Rewards and Recognition

You don't always get the behaviors you really want. But you always get the behaviors people perceive will be rewarded.

—Steve Kerr, *professor at the University of Michigan and adviser to GE's Jack Welch*

Rewards and recognition are the real test of whether Western firms embrace a new management style. Of course, tinkering with rewards can be very dangerous. Roger Stotz, vice president of Maritz, Inc., a noted compensation consulting firm, likes to say, "Rewards are like fire. They keep you warm or burn you."[1]

The problem is that the current system is not working. Base pay ends up putting everyone in higher and higher brackets, and no one ends up getting a significant increase. Merit pay leads to distortions in performance appraisals, and as job security declines with downsizing programs and flattening hierarchies, promotion opportunities become more scarce. The current system, now outdated, focuses on motivating individuals to perform within prescribed boundaries of a job, a department, or a function. Rarely is a contribution to the quality of the whole process a basis for reward and recognition. Despite this, there is only isolated evidence that companies have made a clean break with old conventions of reward and recognition—or of entrenched compensation schemes.

When the defense electronics division at Texas Instruments

set out to reorganize its business, one of the target areas was the reward systems. "We found the system heavily oriented to individual rewards," said Fred Eintracht who heads up the division's high-performing-organizations initiative. "We had annual reviews which affected a person's merit based pay, an employee recognition bonus, a quality award, a perfect attendance recognition, and to acknowledge seniority we offered service recognition, vacations, and parking spots." And when it came to teaming, "the best we had was a monthly quality trophy and a quarterly luncheon for a deserving group."[2]

A wide array of factors are converging to force a redesign of reward and recognition systems in large firms: customer demands, complexity, flattening and downsizing, accelerated rates of knowledge, and skill obsolescence. At the same time, teams are becoming the preferred means of implementing solutions. Agile and flexible teaming and acquiring knowledge quickly are what corporations want from their workers. When all is said and done, the old career track is not there anymore.

> Agile and flexible teaming and accelerated knowledge acquisition are what corporations want from their workers. When all is said and done, the old career track is not there anymore.

There are three avenues to rewarding teams: (1) maintain individual performance ratings and add in an element to account for a person's contribution to his or her team, (2) make a group jointly accountable for a result and still emphasize individual performance evaluations, or (3) make the team the central and primary focus of a reward system. Although the solution should fit the circumstances, it is not a black-and-white choice between teams and individuals. The issue is finding the right mix.

> Although the solution should fit the circumstances, it is not a black-and-white choice between teams and individuals. The issue is finding the right mix.

Two main themes emerge from best practices in rewards and recognitions. One is to shrink individual base pay and increase the percentage that is "pay at risk": a percentage of the employee's salary that will be paid in proportion to a precisely defined target figure. The other is to increase pay for acquired skills or knowledge. And a new goal-sharing paradigm being applied in other corporations provides gains for both the corporation and the individual if performance improves. These systems move away from an entitlement of full pay to variable pay for performance; from individuals to company-wide teams; from exclusively executives having pay at risk to all salaried employees; from position-based to skill-based pay; and from task only to the total process or project as a performance criterion. These practices give employees far more latitude in determining how they will affect performance.

Let us return to the three-tiered system of metrics, introduced in Chapter 7. The cascading flow from objectives, to performance gaps, and to targeted action metrics is an innovation for use in conjunction with a reward and recognition program. Its performance-gap centerpiece pioneered by Analog Devices, is a method of measurement that is missing in many reward and recognition schemes. By defining gaps that must be narrowed consistently over time, they provide a measurement against which to judge performance and against which to assign team accountability. Without these gaps, working teams have no way of establishing whether their efforts directly affect business objectives, such as market share or profitability. Once performance gaps are established, teams can more easily diagnose the barriers they need to attack in order to narrow a particular gap.

How much does one allocate as a financial reward? Susan Cohen, an academic expert on reward systems from the University of Southern California, reports studies showing a percentage threshold above which individuals or groups are motivated by variable pay and below which it makes no difference. That reward threshold is roughly 10 percent of base pay. In other words, "If you're going to dangle a small amount of money, why should I bother?" In practice, companies are offering a broad disparity of variable-pay percentages. Some, like Lotus, offer 25 to 35 percent of base pay; others offer various amounts, still below the threshold 10 percent but moving higher. In 1992, 30 percent of U.S. companies offered a payout averaging 6.2 percent of base pay; by 1994 the numbers jumped to almost 36 percent of companies and an average payout of 7.3 percent.[3]

Corning found that its plant-level staff were highly motivated, even if below the 10 percent threshold, as long as the earned amount is only paid once or twice a year. The single larger lump sum has a greater psychological impact than many smaller monthly amounts might. This method of payment may, in fact, confirm Cohen's judgment that the single lump sum may be *perceived* as more than 10 percent of the month's salary in which it is received and therefore acts as a strong motivator.

"We are the first company to fully implement group variable pay," says H. N. "Rug" Altmansberger, director of goal-sharing at Corning. His lessons learned from three years of instituting the program are summarized in three words: "Communicate, communicate, communicate. Our real task is to get everyone focused on key measures that will meet long-term business goals."[4] His advice underscores how important widespread understanding of the new reward formula is to success in attaining the team's goals. Without it, employees will resist out of fear of losing out and will slowly lose their motivation.

Goal sharing was established in a 1989 pilot program at the company's Blacksburg site. The variable-pay plan is divided into two components: one based on management-established performance criteria such as return on investment and another based on performance criteria established by a team. The pay is calculated according to a quantifiable result, such as yield or output, with pay rewards based on whether 85 percent, 100 percent, 125 percent, or higher targeted goals are achieved. The actual formula is illustrated in Exhibit 12-1. Five criteria are listed to the left, with a weight for each one. The top row of the matrix indicates what percentage of the goal was accomplished, with 100 percent in the middle. Targeted goals are listed within the matrix. For example six patents would be right on target. At the bottom is the payout value. If the 100 percent patent target was reached, the payout would be 5 percent times the weighted value of 5 percent, for a total (top right) of 0.25 percent.

Exhibit 12-1. Corning's formula for goal sharing.

Goalsharing Measure	Weight	40	60	80	100	120	140	160	180	200	Example*
Glass-Polymer Patents	5%	3	4	5	6	7	8	9	10	11	0.25
Customer Deliverables	10%	4	6	8	10	12	14	16	18	20	0.50
Process Development	10%		3		6		7		8	10	0.50
Strategic Business Goals	25%		2		3		4		5	6	1.25
ROE%	50%	14.5	15.0	15.5	16.0	16.5	17.0	17.5	18.0	18.5	3.00
		2%	3%	4%	5%	6%	7%	8%	9%	10%	
TOTAL PAYOUT											5.50

*Example: If 100 percent Goals are met and ROE is at 16.5 percent, Payout will be 5.5 percent.

Source: H. N. Altmansberger.

Another unique feature of Corning's system is the allocation of 1 percent of the base pay to be paid out as spot awards to individuals or teams. The supervisor can make the award with only one approval signature based on above-and-beyond performance. The ground rule is that the check must be in the next payroll cycle after the approval and that the total spot awards not exceed 8 percent of an individual's annual salary. In any given year 15 to 30 percent of employees receive spot bonuses. At Blacksburg, overall performance rates rose sharply over three years from 38 to 85 percent better in each of the four categories earmarked for improvement.

At Lotus, a Cambridge-based software company, a reward program is tailored to product development. It contains two innovations: a very high variable base percentage, putting 25 to 35 percent of base pay at risk, and three measures identified as a basis for the reward: (1) timeliness of shipment, (2) quality of product measured in after-shipment bugs, and (3) marketplace acceptance. The last was possible without serious time lags because feedback in the commercial software business is quick. "We wait for the first reviews in the magazines," said Jim Rickard, U.S. compensation manager for Lotus Development Corporation. Compensation is paid in cash or incentive stock options. The company acknowledges that when it put this plan together, it made a fundamental mistake (which it was quick to correct): The variable pay was at first presented to employees in a formula that appeared to turn it into an entitlement. In other words, project teams quickly came to expect the extra pay just for effort, and not because the product succeeded. That was soon changed by making it explicit that variable pay would be linked to performance results.

At Textron Defense, a large defense-oriented Massachusetts firm facing deep cuts in defense expenditures, it was determined that the traditional two-boss matrix system, a DOD legacy, was too expensive a way to manage a corporation. In 1992, the company turned to a horizontal teaming structure and with it a new reward system. Its main feature is base pay for individual skills and variable pay for team accomplishments. Said Wayne Hellman, the company's executive for organizational redevelopment,

We divided skills into three categories: problem solving, decision making, and interpersonal. To do this we work with product team leaders to determine the capabilities and competencies required. This allows us to identify key skills necessary for us to be proficient and then overlay individuals against those capabilities. In this manner skills needs are better understood and a plan devised with incentives for individuals to up-skill themselves.[5]

Teams develop three to five goals and performance targets. Based on the team's performance, equal lump sums are paid to everyone on the team. A parallel program for key individual contributors was expanded with nonfinancial recognition in the form of certificates, celebrations, and public recognition. The most coveted form of recognition is the Excalibur Award for high performers: pictures and plaques hung in the main lobby near a huge Arthurian stone with a sword thrust in its center.

To Hellman the results have far exceeded expectations. His principal evidence is a sales growth rate that counters the downturn in defense contracts. "After one year," he reports, "teams are performing at improvement rates in the 123 percent to 135 percent range, corporate sales are up by 7 percent—even in the defense downturn—and net operating profit is up 7 percent." If anything has gone wrong, it is success. One of the first issues to arise came from the company's security guards, who wanted to be able to have a chance at shared benefits. They felt that they played an important role in maintaining the security of various teams' operations and thus deserved a share of the pot. A compromise was arrived at.

Texas Instruments settled on a compensation system that offered a 15 percent payout, half based on pay for knowledge and another half based on pay for performance. "With one we want to promote continuous learning as well as breadth of knowledge," stated Eintracht. "With the other we want to get teams to focus on sight goals and a direct link between effort and results." The knowledge component was divided into four topic areas and three levels of competence: strategic knowledge, coordination knowledge, and support knowledge such as basic administrative procedures. The matrix of 20 possible skill areas offered ample room for an individual to advance according to his or her preferences but always consistently with the division's strategic line of sight. For team-based performance pay, a variety of measurements were devised, one of them entitled "flexibility" and measured as the number of different tasks performed by the team divided by the percentage of capable operators in operations. The smaller the denominator is, the higher the reward.

"Whatever you do," says Roger Stotz of the Maritz compensation consulting company, "the reward system should support the strategy." One way he crystallizes this notion is with a simple matrix that aligns reward systems against organizational objectives. Positive and negative correlation values are given at each intersection and quickly reveal whether a set reward system reinforces a corporate objective. "Many times," says Stotz, "to the surprise of the company, there turns out to be absolutely no positive correlation." He goes a step further with a second matrix aligning types of rewards against the financial and psychic values they offer the recipient, as well as performance effects they may induce. This quick analysis can also be revealing if it shows little correlation between a reward system and the value associated with it or the performance effects it tends to induce. The main point, he makes, is that a reward system must be seen and analyzed in a total context. In other words, you get what you pay for. And this is what is perceived will be rewarded.

Notes

1. Roger Stotz, presentation to the IAPD, June 16–18, 1993.
2. Fred Eintracht, presentation to the IAPD, June 16–18, 1993.
3. "Bonus Pay: Buzzword or Bonanza," *Business Week*, November 14, 1994, p. 64.
4. H. N. Altmansberger, presentation to the IAPD, June 16–18, 1993.
5. Wayne Hellman, presentation to the IAPD, June 16–18, 1993.

Chapter 13

Knowledge Management

In the world of self-organizing structures, we learn that useful boundaries develop through openness to the environment. As the process of exchange continues between the system and environment, the system, paradoxically, develops greater freedom from the demands of its environment.

—Margaret Wheatley, *Leadership and the New Science* (1993)

Knowledge is the set of experiences, assumptions and rules that allow you to interpret and act on information. It is only at this stage of the full informational progression that business advantage can be gained.

—Eric P. Dion, *presentation to Groupware 95, Boston*

More and more companies are finding it essential to communicate, share documents, and make decisions in real time. As a consequence, knowledge management has surfaced as a vital aspect of any organization's competitive ability, especially in product development. One solution is to use virtual local area networks (LANs), which

allow companies to form workgroups on the fly. This approach not only lets users share network resources but also provides dedicated band-width to each group. This is accomplished without flooding other parts of the corporate network with broadcast traffic that's intended solely for other members of the same group. . . .

In a number of organizations, it probably makes sense to form a product development team that includes a system engineer, a design engineer, a product marketing person, and someone responsible for the financial management of the project. This group of folks can be scattered throughout the organization, but they need to share information. . . .

Rather than physically reconfiguring the network at the hub by moving cables around, administrators can define and create groups in software by issuing commands from a central management console.[1]

Information accessibility is critical early in the development cycle, when ideas are being loosely formed based on information gathered from a multitude of sources within and outside a company (see Exhibit 13-1 on page 178). This is the front end of product development during which product definition is settled. For this to be managed effectively, teams cannot wait for information; they need real-time access to information.

Once the team has defined a product idea, it enters a *knowledge intensive* phase, in which it engages in problem solving, designing, and testing ideas. During this period, applying organizational and personal knowledge for both creative problem solving and decision making is critical. Collaboration, often aided by electronic support tools, is the human side of knowledge management. Wherever knowledge may reside—in a single individual, in a database, or in an ability of a group to brainstorm together—the key is to make it accessible.

Once the product is developed and put into production, a new level of information exchange takes place; the primary concern is the production, delivery, and tracking of materials, goods, and services. This *transactional logistics* phase involves training, service support, billing, order taking, and production. In most world-class companies, transactional logistics are managed in real time. Data become accessible for decision-making purposes as they are generated. By bringing client and provider in direct contact, the middleman is eliminated from the process.

Michael Schrage, an innovative thinker from Massachusetts Institute of Technology's Media Lab, says that the purpose of knowledge is to "enhance the ability of the expert" and to make that ability accessible to anyone else who needs it. The challenge, therefore, is to manage knowledge—and its accessibility with new electronic tools—through the stages of the product development process.[2]

> The purpose of knowledge management is to "enhance the ability of the expert" and to make that ability accessible to anyone else who needs it.

Consider the case of a company offering a complex service to a large corporate client—perhaps a software solution to a problem or a complicated insurance program to several thousand employees. What if the client calls the parent company? Who answers, and how much will that person know? A customer service representative, for example, will rarely be able to respond without additional help and support because information about the customer may be located in any of several dozen databases that do not talk to one another. At companies like AT&T, information about large customers is stored on 126 mainframe systems. To answer basic questions, service representatives need to access 20 to 25 of these systems, one at a time. At Ford Motor, a senior engineer estimated that there are 3,000 to 5,000 stand-alone systems, none of which "talks" to the next.[3] These are termed *legacy systems*, meaning that they have been inherited from mainframe days, and the cost of tying all of them together is considered prohibitive. Yet by maintaining these separate systems, firms are fragmenting their knowledge and making it difficult—if not impossible—to leverage that knowledge to competitive advantage. AT&T has made it a priority to weave these legacy systems into a seamless whole.

This sort of problem is particularly onerous when it comes to product development. At Pitney Bowes, Al Schmidt, director of operations and technology development, realized that he had a problem on his hands when he and his staff mapped the company's computer support system for product development. What emerged was a network of islands of information that were largely unconnected and required several repetitive manual data entries to record critical information in the right places. He called this way of doing things the "sneaker net," because people literally had to run around and manually make incompatible systems work together. That was in 1992. Three years later, he had engineered an almost complete transition toward a seamless integration of product generation and supply processes, with these benefits:

- Easy flow of mechanical designs across the entire company
- Concurrent activities by mechanical, engineering, and manufacturing
- Lower-cost manufacturing systems
- Reduced time cycles for engineering changes
- Common configuration control
- Uniform performance metrics

These benefits were, in effect, the outcome of a focused attempt at knowledge management. At the core was a simple design principle: a single point source for locating information. One of the best examples of this principle is Ingersoll Milling Machine Company, a maker of giant machine tools in Rockford, Illinois, with 4,200 employees. According to George Hess, vice president for systems and planning, "We now have a central data base that we access 10 million times per shift. This gives us on-line inquiry capability with touch screens located directly in our customers' plants."[4] A customer can enter Ingersoll's database at any time and track in real time the status of its machine order, to the minute and hour. "Our goals were and are simply," states Hess, "to satisfy our customers by profitably producing the best machine tools in the world, to be a low cost producer and to deliver on time."

The single-point design principle was applied in building the architecture necessary to integrate the enterprise electronically. By this, says Hess,

We mean integrating all functions from the proposals to the customer and the comprehensive customer master file, all the way through receipt of order, engineering design, release to manufacturing, procurement of materials, machining of parts, sub-assembly, final assembly, test, field installation, cost tracking, purchasing, inventory, accounts receivable, CAD, CAM, and comprehensive management reporting for all these functions.

Not many other companies have achieved this goal as seamlessly as Ingersoll has. In Hess's view, the competitive benefits have kept the company alive and thriving through the worst of times in the generally troubled machine tool systems industry.

Another case is Levi Strauss, the famed blue jean company that strengthened ties to its supplier base using a system called LeviLink. Electronic media are used to speed up and simplify the entire process of ordering, stocking, receiving, analyzing sales, and making payments for Levi products. The company had two objectives: to increase sales with lower inventory and improve service to retailers. As a result of the system put into place, sales increased 25 percent, and inventory decreased 25 percent. Similar goals are in store for other key processes at Levi Strauss.

> The bottom line to these examples is that all who need to know have access and connectivity with as little fuss or difficulty by all who need to know.

The bottom line of these examples is that all who need to know have access and connectivity with as little fuss or difficulty as possible. In 1989, Robert Johansen and his colleagues at the Institute for the Future in Palo Alto introduced the schematic framework of connectivity and accessibility that lies behind these examples.[5] Their model (Exhibit 13-1) categorizes the tools necessary to support communication and interaction among members of groups or teams. It distinguishes between two variables that come into play: time and place. The holy grail of this model is for teams at the center to be able to communicate to anybody, at any time, and in any place so that any member can

Exhibit 13-1. A framework for connectivity and accessibility.

Groupware Classifications

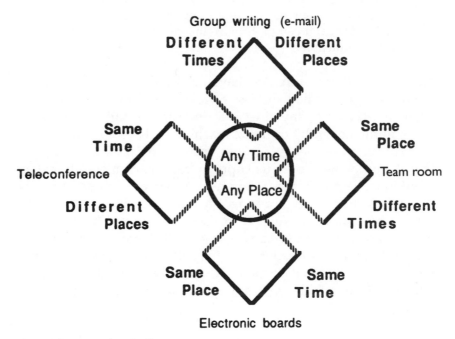

Source: Institute for the Future.

tap the talent and resources of colleagues in real time whenever needed.

Technology is moving fast enough to bring the holy grail to reality. The extreme case, of course, is a virtual enterprise operating with a small core group linked electronically to its suppliers and customers. In such an environment, the individual takes on a completely different character. There is little or no hierarchy, rewards are based more on the freedom to work on what one is interested in, and value is based on merging competencies of various other individuals and their organizations. The rapid evolution of the Internet is bringing many such burgeoning organizations into being.

What "anytime/anyplace" companies look like in reality is

far from a fantasy. One example is KPMG–Peat Marwick, a $6 billion a year firm formerly engaged in accounting and now additionally highly involved in consulting. It has 1,100 offices, worldwide operations, and 76,000 employees. "We are the quintessential knowledge-based company," states Allan Frank, national partner in charge of enabling technologies. Although the firm is engaged principally in consulting, its engagements are analogous to product development in that complex customer needs must be quickly assessed and analyses and solutions provided within short time frames—several weeks to several months. A crucial competitive advantage, explained Frank, is the firm's ability to tap the competence of skilled specialists wherever they might be at any time. "When I meet a client," said Frank, "I should be able to represent the whole firm's capabilities and, in real time, access anyone anywhere to tackle specific subjects. I can now do this from my laptop and a phone line in direct answer to a client's question."

To do this Frank helped conceive and engineer a global restructuring of the giant firm and developed a real-time communication system. The organizational structure is based on 1,100 regional offices, each with diversified capabilities, linked together on a global scale. The link is established by the use of a versatile and cost-effective groupware application called First Class.

Frank's goal was "to take the intellectual assets of the firm and bring them to one point, a single individual." With a laptop as the interface and a network of servers linked together with First Class, he constructed a real-time environment labeled the "Knowledge Manager," which has the following objectives:

- Support development of a virtual global practice.
- Enable collaborative work by geographically dispersed, multidisciplinary teams.
- Share knowledge across geographic boundaries.
- Leverage existing strengths among national and regional practices.
- Support services to national clients.
- Connect the world of online information: commercial databases, the Internet, public news, public e-mail.

"The desire and ability to connect is very organic," remarks Frank. "But connecting them in cyberspace is an even more powerful idea." This was achieved with an initial pilot effort costing no more than an estimated $100,000 and a deployment of user licenses for single-seat costs of $15 to $20.

| The goal: To take the intellectual assets of the firm and bring them to one point, a single individual. |

"The whole process has been organic," states Frank. "Our whole approach has been to seed the organization with a resource [First Class] and to just let it take root on its own." Success of his organic model is tracked by the increases in individual user accounts that have mounted from 400 in October 1993 to 1,400 a year later; total logged hours jumped 600 percent, from 1,000 hours to 7,000 hours in the same period. No one has measured the actual value derived from these new hours of interaction, but the assumption is that it represents new value-adding activity to the company. "Group knowledge is the goal." In Frank's view, common knowledge enhances teamwork and enables complex group action. If the tools are right, people will gravitate naturally to them because they enhance their abilities. This contrasts with tools that are much more structured and are often rigidly imposed on an organization from the top. While such tools may work in enterprises that are largely transaction minded, such as Wal-Mart or Federal Express, they work less well in situations that require individual initiative within more loosely structured teams. The primary vehicle for organically building group know-how at KPMG is the building of "shared conference" files that aggregate documents and exchanges of ideas. Chat boxes allow group to dialogue electronically in real time. Following are some key features of the Knowledge Manager system:

- Teams "own" their conferences. This leads to self-organizing content—not top-down structures and procedures. Everyone learns by using the system.
- Core knowledge may reside at any single geographic site but is accessible in real time to any other site.

- Eighteen servers contain all the firm's knowledge, accessible in real time to 18,000 U.S. users. There are no charges to enter or use content.
- The server is a conceptual reservoir accessible through different paths.
- Knowledge is organized in seven content categories with 31 subheadings.
- Help wanted on specific topics is the most popular conference type. It allows individuals to tap the knowledge of the whole organization and to solve problems much faster and more cost-effectively than before.

These characteristics of the Knowledge Manager, which have helped to build an organization with a living institutional memory, are an outcome, too, of considerable reengineering of the company's internal business processes. "Business process reengineering forces people to look at their organization in a very different way," reflected Frank. "You get to a networked process view. Groupware is linked to this mindset."

This view is echoed by Harry Lasker, a founding partner of Renaissance Strategy Group. The firm has made a quick inroad into the mainstream of consulting practices by stressing the important link between business process reengineering and knowledge management. "A critical piece often missing in reengineering programs," he suggests, "is the understanding that a lot more judgment is being put into the hands of far fewer people. Supporting them at critical decision-making moments is vital." This support comes back to the design principle of a single point source for locating useful information.

"Portable documents are the key," states Eric Dion of Mobil. "They represent a new class of groupware. As 'electronic paper' these formats preserve the look and feel of the original copy—including font and graphic information—and allow documents to be viewed, printed, and duplicated regardless of the computer platform to which the document is sent." While not editable in the copied form, these documents become accessible to wide numbers of people. They stand head and shoulders above e-mail and its crude interfaces as "containers of knowledge" in Dion's words.

In many organizations, product development teams are geographically distributed and need real-time access to similar documents and data. Out of this ability has come the term *collaboratories*, coined by the Institute for the Future and building into a single word the idea of colocation, laboratories, and collaboration. "People are less shy and more playful in electronic discussions," state Lee Sproull and Sara Kiesler. "They also express more opinions and ideas and vent more emotions."[6] From a study of Tandem and its use of electronic communications between team members, they concluded that "askers often admit their ignorance to perhaps hundreds or even thousands of people." Given the growing robustness of group-based electronic tools, the collaboratory is fast finding a natural home in the product development world.

The concept is being put into practice by Lucasfilm in the making of the fourth of its Star Wars series. "The idea is for every individual in the creative and production process—including writers, picture editors and sound technicians—to be able to pitch in, no matter where they are physically situated. 'It's what we call the virtual studio,' " said Gordon Radley, president of Lucasfilm.[7]

> What appears to be happening is a paradoxical combination of centralization and decentralization.

The collaboratory is built on electronic connections that provide video contact, real-time exchanges of voice and data, shared access to a corporate "knowledge reservoir," and tools for group problem solving. "What appears to be happening," write Thomas Malone and John Rockart of MIT, "is a paradoxical combination of centralization and decentralization. Because information can be distributed more easily, people lower in the organization can now become well enough informed to make more decisions more effectively." At the same time, "upper-level managers can more easily review decisions at lower levels."[8] This has the effect of changing power relationships by distributing it to teams low in the organization but still reserving decision-making control at critical points at the top. The electronic systems is a key control and communication mechanism of the three-tiered organization.

Notes

1. Salvatore Salamone, "Virtual LAN's Get Real," *Byte* (May 1995): 181.

2. Michael Schrage, *Shared Minds* (New York: Random House, 1990).

3. Hans Kushnerus, presentation to the IAPD, March 1995.

4. George Hess, presentation to the IAPD, March 1994.

5. Robert Johansen et al. *Leading Business Teams* (Reading, Mass.: Addison-Wesley, 1991), and Robert Johansen, *Groupware: Computer Support for Business Teams* (New York: Free Press, 1988).

6. Lee Sproull and Sara Kiesler, "Computers, Networks and Work," *Scientific American* (September 1991).

7. "Digital Innovator Pays a Price for Being First," *New York Times*, February 1, 1995, p. D4.

8. Thomas W. Malone and John F. Rockart, "Computers, Networks, and the Corporation," *Scientific American* (September 1991).

PART THREE

Scientists *come in two types*. Scientists *of the first type see the world as being basically in equilibrium. And if untidy forces push a system slightly out of equilibrium, then they feel the whole trick is to push it back again.*

Scientists of the second type, however, see the world as a process of flow and change, with the same material constantly going around and around in endless combinations.

—M. Mitchell Waldrop
Complexity

Chapter 14

Continuous Change

*In neolithic times progress occurred over millennia;
two thousand years ago it occurred over centuries.
Today, radical changes can occur in one decade. Indeed,
just as change itself is natural to life, so is the accelera-
tion of change.*

—Peter Russell and Roger Evans
The Creative Manager (1992)

We started this book by making the case that change is continuous. Nowhere else is this more visible, in our view, than in the
day-to-day world of new-product development. The luxury, real
or illusory, of long intervals of equilibrium is long gone. But
competing successfully involves much more than creating new
products. It requires never-ending improvements to strategies,
processes, people's skills, and organizational structures. The
best companies keep all four in balance, and they keep the basics
simple.

Paul Allaire, Xerox's Chairman and CEO, expressed this
succinctly:

> Until recently, Xerox was no different. In the 1980s, we went
> through a number of reorganizations. But none of them got
> at the fundamental question of how to run the company. The
> change we are making now is more profound. We have em-
> barked on a process to change completely the way we man-
> age the company. Changing the structure is only part of that.
> We are also changing the processes by which we manage,
> the reward systems and other mechanisms that shape those

processes, and the kind of people we place in key managerial positions. Finally, we are trying to change our informal culture—the way we do things, the behaviors that drive the business. In fact, the term "reorganization" doesn't really capture what we are trying to do at Xerox. We are redesigning the "organization architecture" of the entire company.[1]

John Seely Brown, chief scientist and corporate vice president at Xerox, believes that many organizations still harbor an obsolete view of people—a view that values them only for what they can produce with their hands and for their ability to follow instructions. He provides a sports analogy. Football, baseball, and basketball—each has a very different way of using people. In football the plays are planned, the players programmed, and the coaches and quarterback constitute a hierarchy calling the shots. In baseball, the individual players are the stars, and the team seldom becomes something greater than the sum of its parts. But basketball is different. Success depends on improvisation around basic sets of skills in a dynamically fast-changing environment. Today's world of business, fast paced as it is, is far more like basketball. It calls for agile and flexible teaming.

| Success depends on improvisation around basic sets of skills in a dynamically fast-changing environment.

The New Organization

We have suggested in this book that a return to company-wide processes and simpler organizational structures is part of the answer. This is evidenced in a rapid evolution toward flatter hierarchies and greater reliance on teams on the operational front lines. The emergence of what we have termed the three-tier organization manifests this evolution. Senior teams at the top focus on strategic objectives, strategic process teams in the middle focus on how work gets done and on narrowing critical performance gaps, and delivery teams at the bottom tackle the day-to-day work. This is indeed the operational model coming into being at companies like Black & Decker and Sabre Development Services. In each case, this three-tier system is supported by a portfolio of core competencies and skills that represent prized or proprietary competitive advantages. At Chrysler this model has bred enormous benefits that can be measured in speedier product development cycles for new cars and rapid market acceptance.

But new ways breed resistance. "Even subtle resistance . . . can be a problem," writes Anne Fisher of *Fortune* magazine. "Most dissenters won't stand up and shout at you that they hate what you're doing to them and to their comfortable old ways. Instead they will nod and smile and agree with everything you say."[2] Resistance can debilitate the most well-meant change efforts.

In Japan, the most basic threat to change, loss of one's job, has until recently been neutralized in large companies by lifetime employment. Similarly, the threat of reduction in pay or prestige is neutralized by the tradition of pay by seniority and by job rotation and training for new assignments. The role of a Japanese employee in his organization is often explained as being "organic," like a cell within a body. Understanding that the cell atrophies without a vital role to perform, the Japanese employee is rotated through various positions so that he sees the company as a whole. In the process, he can build a personal network within the organization and better find ways of fitting into the whole organization.

Accelerations in the Western corporate rates of change, fueled in large part by an explosion of technological innovations and in part by Japan's dynamic industrial challenges, happened because continuous change was harnessed as a competitive advantage. Motorola's galvanizing "six sigma" program symbolized a never-ending commitment to improvement. For GE, the catalyst was an individual, Jack Welch, relentless in his vision of what could be. At Chrysler, senior management had no choice left but to change or to go out of business. Bailed out by the U.S. government, it scraped its way back to health and used the time it bought to reconstruct completely the way it did business. A serendipitous resource was a cadre of ex–American Motors executives, whose company was bought by Chrysler, and who brought with them survival habits of making cars with small, lean teams. Glenn Gardner, who headed the highly publicized LH platform development team at Chrysler, was one of them. He applied a change strategy with fifteen working principles:

1. Final needs of customer dictate all actions.
2. Quality comes first.
3. Personal goals are second.
4. All non-value-added activity is eliminated.
5. Every employee is empowered to put the customer first (e.g., to take risks).
6. Continuously improve.
7. New timing/scheduling assumptions are made.
8. Suppliers are brought in early and trained.
9. No decision before its time.
10. Value-adding work is on the critical path—not such things as management reviews or approval.
11. Simultaneous engineering and concurrent testing.
12. Decisions pushed to the technical level where the information is.
13. Decisions by consensus of all interfaces in the company.
14. Constantly focus on who pays for the final product.
15. Benchmark against the best of the best.

At the heart of these principles is a firm commitment to continuous change. The outcome is a flatter organization, team-based work, reliance on competencies (not functions), and a will to succeed.[3]

But appearances can be deceptive. Change is not meaningful if it is ordered from the top and confined to redrawing a company's organization and structure. Flatter organizations alone do not mean broader empowerment or that responsibility has been pushed to a lower level. It may mean fewer people burning themselves out trying to make more decisions on less information. In too many companies, we see that well-publicized bold strikes are usually less effective than longer, slower marches that are paced to sustain themselves. In slow marches, the CEO does not command the results; he or she challenges the whole organization to respond. Most likely, the CEO will not control the outcomes. But if the line of sight is kept firm and clear, initial chaos gives way to longer-lasting patterns of behavior that are more likely to affect the culture of the corporation.

In too many companies, we see that well-publicized bold strikes are usually less effective than longer, slower marches that are paced to sustain themselves.

To effect change, "managers need to expand their thinking," say organizational experts Lee G. Bolman of the University of Missouri-Kansas City and Terrence E. Deal of Vanderbilt University. They illustrate the point by contrasting "how managers think" with "how managers *might* think:"[4]

How Managers Think	*How Managers* **Might** *Think*
1. Managers often have limited views of organizations (for example, many attribute most organizational problems to the defects of various individuals and groups).	1. They need a holistic framework that encourages inquiry into a range of significant issues: people, power, structure, and symbols.
2. Regardless of the source of a problem, managers often choose rational and structural solutions: rational discourse, restructuring, facts, and logic.	2. They need a palette that identifies a full array of options: bargaining as well as training, ceremony as well as reorganization.
3. Managers have often been taught to value certainty, rationality, and control, and to shun ambiguity and paradox.	3. Managers need to become more creative and more willing to take risks in response to the dilemmas and paradoxes of organizational life. They need to focus on finding the right questions as much as the right answers, on finding meaning and pattern amidst clutter and confusion.
4. Leaders often try to change organizations by finding the one right answer and the one best way; they are stunned by the turmoil and resistance that they thereby generate.	4. Leaders must be passionately committed to their principles but also flexible in understanding and responding to the events around them.

Change and Product Development

Each one of the four new ways Bolman and Deal propose is critical to the successful development and introduction of new products. Each is a step toward overcoming many of the don'ts summarized in the opening chapters of this book. This still leaves to the CEO and other key executives the need to:

- Communicate a crisp *vision* of the future.
- Establish a *strategy*.
- Set stretch *goals*.
- Motivate people to meet the *goals*.
- *Support and train*.
- Sustain the effort over the *long term*.

Translating goals into meaningful actions for people to take may be one of the most effective change drivers, yet it is rarely well executed. One reason is that senior managers stop short. By simply expressing their objectives, they believe their job is done. Rarely do they transfer the responsibility to process teams of line managers with a companywide perspective. These are the people who can define performance gaps and delegate accountability for direct actions to delivery teams.

| Translating goals into meaningful actions for people to take may be one of the most effective change drivers, yet it is rarely well executed.

Speaking on this point, a manager reflected, "If I had to tell those reporting to me what to do, I would be telling them they were not capable of carrying out their jobs." This style of management is far from the top-down micromanagement of command and control. It is the core behavior of what has come to be expected of world-class companies.

Where does all this lead for the future of product development? As we noted in the first chapters, increasing complexity will lead to greater reliance on integrative process teams as the owners of critical competitive know-how. It will lead, too, to the strengthening of competency centers as the repositories of knowledge. And it will lead to a world of work in which electronic tools provide real-time access to information and know-how, wherever it resides. The hybrid organization flowing out of these trends is the three-tier one we have described. It treats processes such as product development from a systemic perspective and manages them with little regard for artificial barriers to the flow of information. Far from being a fad of the 1990s, it is an organizational solution to managing whole systems fast and flexibly in response to change.

Notes

1. "The CEO as Organizational Architect: An Interview with Xerox's Paul Allaire," *Harvard Business Review* (September–October 1992), p. 108.

2. "Making Change Stick," *Fortune Magazine*, April 17, 1995, p. 124.

3. Glenn Gardner, presentation to the Product Development Management Association, Atlanta, 1993.

4. L. G. Bolman and T. E. Deal, *Reframing Organizations: Artistry, Choice and Leadership* (San Francisco: Jossey-Bass, 1991), p. 18.

Chapter 15
Ten X

Things should be made as simple as possible but not simpler.

—Albert Einstein

Early in this book we observed that a new awareness of the broad systemic span of product development is the real novelty of the 1990s. Those who act systemically outmaneuver and outpace their competition consistently over time. These are the do-loopers. To do so, however, means a relentless chase after 10 × possibilities. Improving by orders of magnitude is nothing less than what is expected of world-class companies.

Although this improvement can be achieved through laboratory breakthroughs or the sheer weight of financial clout, it is more and more evident that the real payoffs are coming from companies that make a fundamental shift in how they manage their resources. As Marvin Patterson of Hewlett-Packard writes:

> A clearly defined strategy—the force field that drives the company forward—is an absolute prerequisite to reduce the time to perceive opportunities. . . . The most productive approach maintains market research as a continuous program in partnership with technology research efforts. . . . With the opportunities already identified, project teams can hit the ground running toward the right opportunity and do not have to waste a moment trying to identify an opportunity themselves. Shortening the investment time means faster time to market, which is really the objective of the whole product development process improvement exercise.[1]

In some of Hewlett-Packard's operations, such as its home and small business inkjet printer group, monthly production rates run at more than 200,000 and are expected to double within a year because of increased rates of new-product introductions and enormous demand. For this segment of HP's business to function, it must design, produce, and fill all its distributor shelves before the first sales promotion campaign starts. If anything is out of sync, a whole selling cycle can be lost because of the rapid obsolescence of these products. "Excellence in execution," says Buck Heidrik, a business process engineer at the company, "becomes highly critical." This cannot be accomplished by piecemealing the process.

> An ability to respond systemically to problems and opportunities is the true differentiator of world-class performance.

This is why we have come to a singular conclusion about the 10 × challenge: An ability to respond systemically to problems and opportunities is the true differentiator of world-class performance. We have characterized this as a commitment to deliver the whole enterprise in the service of the customer. In day-to-day practice, this means an ability to manage all of the parts of an enterprise as a single whole. This, we have found, is what the best strive to do but clearly not the way many of us do it. One need only ask a simple question to put the matter to the test in one's organization: *Who is in charge of product development?* If the answer is the name of a single individual or a single function, as is most often the case, there is little systemic know-how.

The prior chapters built on what is meant by a holistic style of management by outlining best practices that meet this test. New notions of teaming, expressed in cross-organization processes, are one component of that equation. A strategic process focus has, by definition, its eye on fusing all the parts into a single efficient and effective whole. When we spoke of new techniques as simple as mapping a pattern of working relationships among the members of a product development team, the same underlying goal is expressed. A similar theme was at the core of an evolving system of metrics designed to make explicit the relationship between high-level enterprise objectives and the execution of tasks low in the organization. Absent such linkages there can be little systemic understanding of why and how work might best be accomplished. A comprehensive system of measurement and metrics, made precise and unambiguous, brings with it a shared language that can be communicated company-wide.

When we wrote of supplier networks, we pointed to the same holistic theme. The best companies build interlocking networks of complementary capabilities that build on unique strengths. It is clear too that there are no singular silver bullet models. What works in Japan is not what we see working in Silicon Valley or Wales. The same is true of technology management. A market-driven Japanese model of how best to manage research and development is relevant and effective because of its systemic quality. The three-track approach is designed to work as a web of interactions, each reinforcing the next. This contrasts, of course, with a Western predilection to isolate pure researchers and at the other extreme to push untested development ideas faster into product development.

When it comes to a rapidly emerging awareness of knowledge management as a strategic success factor, it becomes evident that the real issue is connectivity. Are people connected to an open information environment that supports knowledge creation and effective decision making? The answer is that the best companies have worked hard, and many successfully so, to create this connectivity. The consulting firm KPMG is an example of a large company that has achieved this worldwide connectivity and made it a competitive advantage. Those that do not function this way operate with a leg short when it comes to leveraging their know-how.

> The most pervasive Western Achilles heel when it comes to acting systemically may be the deeply entrenched reward and recognition systems inherited from a Tayloristic and command-and-control past.

We have concluded that the most pervasive Western Achilles heel when it comes to acting systemically may be the deeply entrenched reward and recognition systems inherited from a Tayloristic and command-and-control past. While this is clearly a frontier ripe for experimentation, it is the single thickest barrier to change still in our path. This is why experiments such as Corning's Goalsharing are so significant. They are changing the way we think about motivation, reward, and careers by making the whole enterprise-wide effort stand more visibly ahead of the narrow departmental or functional mission. And what is more significant in Corning's case is the strong emphasis it has put on recognizing and rewarding individual initiative. These are issues that challenge Japan and Europe too. In Japan, downsizing of firms and a younger generation less loyal to corporate careers are rapidly putting the big company reward of lifelong employment to the test. In Europe, where financial rewards are less of a motivating factor and long vacations are viewed as a basic work right, the search is just beginning for ways in which to stimulate 10 × behavior.

> The more complex the setting is, the simpler are the solutions to its management—hence, the repeated emphasis of the three-tier organization as a basic feature of the emerging lean and flexible do-loop organization.

From this complexity of interwoven characteristics of the world-class company, we have extracted another theme. The more complex the setting is, the simpler are the solutions to its management—hence, the repeated emphasis of the three-tier organization as a basic feature of the emerging lean and flexible do-loop organization. To paraphrase our opening quotation, this is as simple as we would want to make it, and not more. Through this lens we have seen companies experiment with simple working hierarchies in which teams are the primary players. At Chrysler, for example, platform teams hold considerable control over the decisions that must be made in developing new-car models. This has jarred the traditional political turf and changed the rules of the game. These teams, counting up to 700 engineers, reflect the company's knowledge not as a collage of independent functions but as a single colocated operating unit. There, specialized knowledge is nurtured in competency centers and stimulated through participation in technology clubs. The three-tier teaming model is not a blueprint for any and all business enterprises, but it does challenge the viability of older pyramid-like structures with numerous top-down management layers and a multitude of separate but equal entities at the bottom.

It is fitting to end with the words of systems thinker D. L. Meadows:

> As humans create a world of increasingly complex systems, it becomes more important that we be able to formulate views of their operations that are coherent (and holistic). A tool that allows a client to grapple with some of his/her ideas can lead, for example, to the discovery that goals that seemed reasonable when only part of the system was viewed are inconsistent or impossible in the context of the whole system.[2]

For those embarked on the world-class journey, the 10 × challenge is a condition of doing business. It is a journey in which the skills, the resources, and the means are treated as a whole, not as a collage of parts. The result is an organization that communicates and learns seamlessly and effectively across its boundaries, irrespective of status and geography, and delivers the whole of its efforts to its customers.

Notes

1. Marvin L. Patterson, *Accelerating Innovation: Improving the Process of Product Development* (New York: Van Nostrand, 1993), p. 123.

2. John D. W. Morecroft and John Sterman, eds., *Modeling for Learning Organizations* (Portland, OR: Productivity Press, 1994), p. 101.

Appendix A

New Organizational Models and Trends

Edited by Frank Basa for the IAPD

There is an extensive literature and academic interest in the organization and structure of enterprises. It is evident that context is the driver, and form follows. Thus, one does not start by designing a structure and then fit the context to it. As a result, there are many structural variations depending on the industry, market dynamics, and the strategy of the firm. Few articles have made explicit the connection between product development as a strategic process and the structure that can best support it. This research is meant as an overview of the expert views (academic principally) and the current literature. Each of the following sections contains a synopsis and a list of readings.

The Information Processing Model

Information processing models of organization hypothesize that when the processing demands of a task and the processing capacity of an organization or subunit are well matched, performance is highest. For well-defined tasks, more mechanistic and bureaucratic organizations are appropriate because contingencies can be planned for ahead of time. Less well-defined tasks are performed better by a less rigid organization structure that allows for real-time problem solving unencumbered by hierarchical and bureaucratic controls.

If a new circumstance arises in a bureaucracy, this exception can be processed by several mechanisms:

1. It can be refereed up the hierarchy of authority for a decision to be taken.
2. Rules and procedures can be put in place for future similar events.
3. Planning and goal setting can establish targets so decisions can be taken at a lower level in the hierarchy.
4. Spans of control can be narrowed.

These mechanisms are sometimes inadequate, and two basic strategies for organization design are available: reduce the need for information processing or increase the capacity to process information. Reducing the need for information processing can be achieved in the following ways:

1. Managing the environment so fewer demands are made on the organization.
2. Creating slack resources by adding people or by reducing performance levels (i.e., extending schedules).
3. Creating self-contained tasks where each group or division has its own full complement of resources.

Alternatively, the information processing capacity of the organization can be increased in these ways:

1. Investments in vertical information systems that can convey the needed information to points in the hierarchy where it can be analyzed and acted upon without overloading the hierarchy.
2. Creating lateral relations so that coordination across functional areas can be accomplished by people close to the work rather than by people further up the hierarchy. This includes task forces, committees, and matrix arrangements.

Galbraith, Jay, *Designing Complex Organizations*. Reading, MA: Addison-Wesley, 1973.

Galbraith and Mohrman, both at the University of Southern California, have extended this basic theoretical model and now emphasize the importance of lateral mechanisms for coordinating organizations. This model is analogous to the IAPD strawman referred to in the Preface. The following sources contain descriptions of processes in these lateral organizations, as well as case studies of several European firms.

Further Reading

Galbraith, Jay. *The Business Unit of the Future.* CEO Publication G 92–3. April 1992.

————. *New Forms of Organization III.* CEO Publication G 91–8. N.d.

————. *Designing Informal Networks.* CEO Publication G 92–5. April 1992.

————. *Competing with Flexible, Lateral Organizations.* Reading, MA: Addison-Wesley, 1993.

Mohrman, Susan. *The Emerging Prominence of the Lateral Organization.* Publication G 93-1. Center for Effective Organization (CEO). April 1992.

————, Allan Mohrman, and Susan Cohen. *Human Resource Strategies for Lateral Integration in High Technology Settings.* CEO Publication G 91-11. N.d.

New Organizational Forms

The new organizational forms of the future are hard to predict, but several aspects of organizational architecture are likely to be present:

- Autonomous work teams
- High-performance work systems
- Alliances and joint ventures
- Spinouts
- Networks
- Self-designed organizations
- Fuzzy boundaries contributed to by alliances and joint ventures, spinouts, and networks, but also caused by co-operative design with suppliers and customers as well as information systems that cross organizational boundaries
- Teamwork at the top

Nadler, David. "Organizational Architecture: A Metaphor for Change." In Nadler et al., *Organizational Architecture: Designs for Changing Organizations*. San Francisco: Jossey-Bass, 1992.

Network Organizations

These general impressions of what organizations will look like are representative of much writing on the topic of the network organization. They are supported by other writings that focus on one or more aspects from a different, often more detailed perspective, or from specific case studies of organizations.

"A network form is designed to handle tasks and environments that demand flexibility and adaptability. A network organization can flexibly construct a unique set of internal and external linkages for each unique project."

Baker, Wayne. "The Nework Organization in Theory and Practice." In Nitin Nohria and Robert Eccles. *Networks and Organizations: Structure, Form and Action*. Boston: *Harvard Business Press*, 1992.

Network organizations consist of a "fluid, flexible, and dense pattern of working relationships that cut across various intra- and interorganizational boundaries."

Nohria, Nitin, and Robert Eccles. "Face-to-Face: Making Network Organizations Work." In Nohria and Eccles, *Networks and Organizations: Structure, Form and Action*. Boston: Harvard Business Press, 1992.

Macrolevel Network Forms

Hedlund discusses the evolution of multinationals from the end point of a domestic firm (the center) with a small international division through to the heterarchical Multi-National Corporation that is characterized by (1) many centers, (2) corporate-level strategy formulated and implemented in geographically dispersed centers (strategy is not formulated only at the home country center), (3) centers are different and there is no one overriding dimension for defining centers (functions, products, ge-ography, customer type, etc.) that is superordinate to all the rest, (4) there is flexibility in choice of governance modes (i.e., what is internally controlled and externally purchased), (5) integra-tion is achieved primarily through normative control rather than through coercive or bureaucratic mechanisms, and (6) informa-tion about the whole is contained in each part (the organization is a type of hologram where thinking occurs throughout all parts of the organization).

Hedlund, Gunnar. "The Hypermodern MNC: A Heterarchy?" *Human Resource Management* 25 (1986).

The following types of network organization—spider's web, starburst, and shamrock organizations and federal coordi-nation—tend to be flatter than their predecessors and composed of smaller units.

Spider's Web

The spider's web operates with minimal hierarchical control. "Individual units would operate entirely independently if it were not essential to capture certain information economies of scale or scope that benefit the total organization." This form is appropriate when the nodes have significant interdependence. "Unlike the units of infinitely flat organizations, each of the nodes in a spider's web needs, for effectiveness, to be intimately in touch with the information or resources all other nodes may contain" (p. 123). The center, if it exists, "collects and transfers information from and for the nodes, instead of generating it" (p. 121). "When authority interactions are necessary with the cen-ter, they tend ot occur through single-level task forces, ad hoc committees of peers, or an agreed upon coordinating committee for a special purpose like capital allocation" (p. 121).

Examples of spider's webs include international coopera-tive research ventures, research divisions of larger organiza-tions, and legal, investment banking, auditing and other consulting organizations. Skunkworks and cross-functional de-sign teams typify the spider's web. Quinn uses Arthur Andersen as an example.

"The most important key to managing the spider's web—after selection and development of people and the information system itself—is to make sure the incentive structure focuses on the customer and that the organizations internal structures are designed around the twin goals of sharing information and adding value for customers" (p. 124). Managers in these organizations "often consciously leave the formal organization ill-defined, but establish well-defined, customer-oriented control and monitoring systems centering on individual client or segment activities" (p. 125).

"Spider's webs serve best where a high degree of expertise is needed at the nodes, where relations between nodes themselves or between nodes and the center are intermittent and largely informational—or where local flexibility and creativeness are more important than central efficiencies" (p. 128).

Quinn, James Brian. *Intelligent Enterprise: A Knowledge and Service Based Paradigm for Industry.* New York: Free Press, 1992.

Starburst

Starburst organizations continually spin out units that are self-contained and based on free-standing product lines. The goal is to have autonomous units remain innovative and make their own decisions rather than have internal bureaucracies constraining these organizations. The spinouts are linked to the parent by some core competency. Examples of this form are Thermo Electron, Raychem, 3M, Hewlett-Packard, and MCI.

Quinn, James Brian. *Intelligent Enterprise: A Knowledge and Service Based Paradigm for Industry.* New York: Free Press, 1992.

Shamrock Organizations

Shamrock organizations have a small, permanent core that operates primarily as a coordinating body. Work is outsourced to companies that specialize in some particular aspect or phase of activity. The small core is supplemented by temporary workers who are brought on when needed.

"For example, semiconductor chips may be designed almost anywhere, have their photo masks made in Silicon Valley, and be wafer-etched in Japan, diced and mounted in Korea, assembled in Malaysia, encapsulated in Singapore, and finally sold through independent distributors anywhere in the world" (p. 126).

Quinn, James Brian. *Intelligent Enterprise: A Knowledge and Service Based Paradigm for Industry*. New York: Free Press, 1992.

Federalism

As organizations grow larger and more units are added, the core cannot oversee everything, and a federal form emerges. Rather than the center's delegating tasks and duties and authorities to the outlying parts as in decentralization, "the center's powers are given to it by the outlying groups, in a sort of reverse delegation. The center does not direct or control so much as coordinate, advise, influence, and suggest" (p. 118).

"The federal organization is not only different in its form and shape, it is culturally different, it requires a different set of attitudes from those who seek to manage it and from those who are managed. . . . The federal organization will not work unless those in the center not only have to let go of some power but actually want to do so, because only then will they trust the new decision makers to take the right decisions, and only then will they enable them to make them work" (p. 126).

Within this new organization form "the new manager must be a different manager. He, and increasingly she, must use what . . . is called reinforcement theory, applauding success and forgiving failure; he or she must use mistakes as an opportunity for learning. . . . The new manager must learn to specify the measures of success as well as the signs of failure and must allow his or her people the space to get on with it in their own way. The new manager has to be a teacher, counselor and friend, as much as or more than he or she is commander, inspector, and judge. . . . If we cannot do it, then federalism becomes anarchy, control reverts to the center, the center becomes too big and too expensive" (p. 132).

Handy, Charles. *The Age of Unreason*. Boston: Harvard Business Press, 1990.

Single and Multiple Unit Networks

Network organization also exists at the level of a single unit, although some of the forms discussed also apply to organizations composed of multiple units.

Heydebrand defined form in terms of six dimensions: (1) size of labor force, (2) object of labor (e.g., produce commodities, deliver services, or manipulate symbols), (3) means of production, (4) division of labor, (5) control of labor, (6) ownership and control. Postbureaucratic forms "are smaller or are small subunits of larger organizations," staffed by specialists, professionals, and experts who work in an organic, decentralized structure of project teams, task forces, and relatively autonomous groups, have "little emphasis on formal division of labor and managerial hierarchy," comprise a loosely coupled organizational structure that is frequently reorganized, and "require new methods of fostering social cohesion, such as interpersonal relations, clan like norms and practices, and the creation of a corporate culture."

Heydebrand, Wold. *New Organizational Forms.* Work and Occupations 16 (1989).

Mills views hierarchy as nearly dead as a means of coordinating people in organizations. Clusters are the new coordinating mechanism in his model. "Clusters are groups of people drawn from different disciplines who work together on a semipermanent basis. The clusters themselves handle many administrative functions, thereby divorcing itself from an extensive managerial hierarchy. A cluster develops its own expertise, expresses a strong customer or client orientation, pushes decision making toward the point of action, shares information broadly, and accepts accountability for its business results. Typically, a cluster organization subordinates detailed budgets and reporting in favor of broader goals, which are communicated to the organization as a whole. Members of the clusters are expected to understand the broader objectives of the company and to use their imagination and initiative to help accomplish them." Common types of clusters in organizations are core teams, business units, staff units, project teams, alliance teams, and change teams. Mills's examples include the Bay City, Michigan, GM power train plant, Swissair, and British Petroleum. Conrail is another example.

Mills, D. Quinn. *Rebirth of the Corporation*. New York: John Wiley, 1991.

Further Reading

Bahrami, Homa. The Emerging Flexible Organization." *California Management Review* (1991).

Charan, Ram. "How Networks Reshape Organizations—For Results." *Harvard Business Review* (September–October 1991).

Drucker, Peter. "The Coming of the New Organization." *Harvard Business Review* (January–February 1988).

Huber, George. "The Nature and Design of the Post-Industrial Organization." *Management Science* 30 (1984).

Miles, Raymond, and Charles Snow. "Organizations: New Concepts for New Forms." *California Management Review* (Spring 1986).

———. "Causes of Failure in Network Organizations." *California Management Review* (1991).

O'Toole, James, and Warren Bennis. "Our Federalist Future: The Leadership Imperative." *California Management Review*.

Peters, Tom. "Rethinking Scale." *California Management Review*.

New Forms Driven by Information Technology

Although the network organization appears to be the most commonly written about new form, there are other forms and processes that are being discussed.

Infinitely Flat Organization

The infinitely flat is a form enabled largely by information technology. Line managers give few orders, and a central coordinating information resource is present. It is used in fast food organizations for logistics support and in brokerage houses and

by Federal Express to coordinate autonomous units to form co-
herently coordinated overall organization. "By routinizing and
automating operating parameters at their finest replicable level,
both manufacturing and services companies can also develop
the detailed cost and quality controls they need for system coordination and productivity at each of their many highly decentralized operating nodes. Under proper circumstances, the
scheduling, order-giving, and information feedback functions
normally provided by hierarchical structures can be completely
automated" (p. 115).

The infinitely flat form can be used where "(1) localized
interactive contact is important, (2) each ultimate contact point
or operations unit can operate essentially independently from
all the others at its level, (3) the critical relationships between
decentralized units and the center are largely quantitative or informational, and (4) the majority of the relationships with the
information center can be routine or rule-based. . . . The common characteristic of the infinitely flat organization is that interactions occur either at the local contact point or with a
communications center" (pp. 119–120).

Quinn, James Brian. *Intelligent Enterprise: A Knowledge and Service
   Based Paradigm for Industry.* New York: Free Press, 1992.

Further Reading

Short, James, and N. Venkatraman. "Beyond Business Process
   Redesign: Redefining Baxter's Business Network." *Sloan Man-
   agement Review* (Fall 1992).
Walton, Richard. *Up and Running.* Boston: Harvard Business
   Press, 1990.

Dynamically Stable Organization

To cope with the changing nature of the competitive environment and shortened product life cycles, firms need to develop a
set of flexible and responsive process capabilities. The goal is for
the firm to be able to respond flexibly to market demands with
an evolving but relatively stable set of process capabilities. There
are four challenges facing business organizations in redefining

the firm in this fashion: (1) define a path to move the organization from mass production to dynamic flexibility; (2) decouple process know-how capabilities from product and investments from known short-run product requirements; (3) evaluate and deploy the firm's knowledge assets; and (4) identify the firm's real competitors.

Crucial enablers of the dynamically flexible organization are the information systems in place in the organization. These systems are of three types: systems of scope, vertical systems, and horizontal systems. *Systems of scope* distribute information to managers throughout the organization. Often knowledge is present in an organization, but the people who could use it do not know it is available. *Vertical systems* carry specific data to parts of the hierarchy where the data can be used in decision making. *Horizontal systems* are the tool that managers use to coordinate and control process capabilities that cut across functions and departments in the organization. ABB is an example of the dynamically stable organization.

Further Reading

Boynton, Andrew, and Bart Victor. "Beyond Flexibility: Building and Managing the Dynamically Stable Organization." *California Management Review* (Fall 1991).

Boynton, Andrew. "Achieving Dynamic Stability Through Information Technology." *California Management Review* (Winter 1993).

Lattice Organization

The prime (and only) example is W. L. Gore and Associates. The organization has almost no formal structure. It runs primarily on informal networks and a strong culture. People are expected to seek out ways to help the company and are "indoctrinated" and monitored by a sponsor in the organization. Objectives are set by those who do the work and have to make things happen. "The structure within the lattice is described by the people at Gore as complex and evolves from interpersonal interactions, self-commitment to group-known responsibilities, natural leadership, and group imposed discipline."

Shipper, Frank, and Charles Manz. "Employee Self-Management Without Formally Designated Teams: An Alternative Road to Empowerment." *Organizational Dynamics* (1992).

Types of Innovative Organizations

Large System Technology Producers: AT&T, Boeing, Oil Companies

Because of the large investments required (billions of dollars) these organizations tend to perform systemwide innovation rather gradually. They emphasize getting it right the first time rather than speed.

Basic Research Companies: Merck, Hoffman-LaRoche

Firms invest in risky long-term basic research. These firms tend to be careful before committing to development, especially large-scale phase III clinical trials, because of the significant resources that are needed for development. Careful assessment of the market and probability of success is undertaken to guide decision making.

Dominant-Market-Share-Oriented Companies: Matsushita, IBM

They are not first to adopt radical new technologies because they do not want to cannibalize their own sales in established markets. They maintain basic research to keep an eye on what is coming over the horizon. Significant effort is made in market research to define price-performance windows so that as a market emerges, they can use their distribution networks to invade the market. These firms tend to have significant production capacity and are frequently low-cost and high-quality producers. They use market power, incremental improvements to their products, and phased new-product release strategies to overwhelm smaller, innovative state-of-the-art producers.

State-of-the-Art Producers: Cray, Genentech, Kyocera

Technology units are frequently devoid of or detached from formal maketing units. The driving force in the markets these firms service is technical performance of the product. These units frequently need to purchase access to assets they do not possess in order to enter the market (marketing and sales force, large scale clinical testing expertise, etc.).

Discrete Freestanding Product Lines: 3M, Raychem, Thermo Electron

Entrepreneurial spinoffs are established to develop a specific technology that is derived from the center companies' core technological capability, for the market. These firms may not perform careful market research before introducing the product. Market knowledge is often gained by trial and error.

Limited Volume or Fashion Companies: Designer Clothing, Military Hardware, Building

Prototypes, sketches, and mock-ups are put together by individuals or small teams and presented to possible customers for feedback. Reiterative design leads to the final product. Specialized skill in production technology, artistic design, and interpreting feedback from potential customers are usually needed to make this type of innovation successful.

"One-Off" Job Shops: ASIC design houses, software

Specialized knowledge of these firms is used in concert with sophisticated customer inputs to produce customized products for the customer.

Appendix B

Enabling Hierarchies

Pat C. Hoy II

Presentation to the IAPD on organization and structure

Just a little less than a year earlier, I had graduated from the United States Military Academy at West Point—a new second lieutenant, perhaps more experienced than most. I had served during my senior year as a company commander with supervisory responsibility for about 125 cadets from all four classes—plebes, yearlings, cows, and firsties, they were called—in a class system that made it easy to deal with everyone except my own classmates, the seniors. Getting my own classmates to do willing and cheerfully what I wanted them to do, and failing on occasion, had taught me unforgettable lessons and given me high hopes.

But I had spent the year since graduation learning to be a field artilleryman, five months at Fort Sill, Oklahoma, mastering one firing system, and four at Fort Bliss, Texas, mastering another—howitzers and missiles. The days had been long and boring, and the eight weeks in Georgia following those two technical schools offered excitement and relief, even if jumping out of airplanes meant becoming a plebe again. But floating through the humid Georgia air beneath a silk parachute was quite different from days on the bayonet course, and when I finally touched terra firma, it was a blessing, more like a soft kiss on the ass of a three-point landing than a combat zone in Normandy.

When I walked into Captain Al Maddox's office, following all those schools and all that jumping, I still hadn't been prepared for the greeting. I showed up an immaculate conception in a brand new set of hand-tailored army greens, the best hat money could buy, a pair of genuine leather shoes shined to high heavens, and a salute so practiced it had become as natural as breathing—a cultivated sign of civility that carried with it an unspoken but deep-seated respect for a profession that dared show such hierarchical courtesies—top down and bottom up. Saluting, in those pre-Vietnam days, was a privilege and a greeting. I knocked on Captain Maddox's door, positioned myself squarely in front of his desk, stood elegantly, if I do say so myself, at attention, and rendered a hand salute.

"Sir, Lieutenant Hoy, reports for duty."

Maddox looked up from his work without a word. I could see him sizing me up as he sucked air through his teeth and pushed himself back into his chair and away from his desk until he had it just right in his mind what he would say to me. He didn't get up; he didn't extend his hand in courtesy; he didn't even return my salute.

"Second Lieutenant," he said finally, rubbing in the *Second,* "I see you're a West Pointer and you've just come from airborne school."

"Yes sir," I said trying to enter a conversation.

"The only thing you've got going for you is, you didn't go Ranger. I'd like you to rewrite the site security plan and in a week or two, we'll see whether you're ready to take over the launcher platoon from Lieutenant McGance. Any questions?"

"No sir," I said, as I saluted and made my way out of his office and into a new life.

At a very young age, I had to learn to stand up to Al Maddox's authority without compromising my own integrity and without doing damage to the unit we'd been commissioned to lead. It was there in Charlie Battery that I began to form a notion about organizations that I would not understand for nearly thirty years. What kept me in the dark so long was the hierarchy itself. I lived inside it all those years without realizing that it had allowed me to survive Al Maddox, and it had allowed Charlie Battery to be an award-winning unit, even with a son-of-a-bitch in command.

I had to go to Harvard to understand that lesson about hierarchies. I was there following a twenty-eight-year army career that included combat in Vietnam and fourteen years as a tenured professor on the West Point faculty. At Harvard, I worked for Al Maddox's avatar, a self-important southerner who had come East a needy man and stayed that way for almost fifteen years. Working for him, I came to understand something about the power of enabling hierarchies, but I didn't learn it directly from him.

Harvard is a loose federation of minds, a group of brilliant individuals isolated from one another by the very acts of mind that make the place a great university. No one can be around Harvard long without experiencing bouts of insecurity in the face of astonishing performances by so many gifted people. But the faculty isolates itself in its work. Those in positions of leadership seem to know almost nothing about enabling hierarchies. Because they have long been caught up and consumed in a world of their own idea making, they have been denied a lasting return on communal investments. The reality of shared responsibility and teamwork is as hard to experience at Harvard as unfettered freedom is at West Point.

At West Point, from day one—even as cadets are learning to stand up under the most grueling individual tests—they are always investing themselves in each other's lives. They repeat over and over their mantra of survival. Cooperate and graduate. Cooperate and graduate. Few believe they can make it alone. Those who try usually fail. A lone rifleman does not wage war and win.

Within those hierarchies, men (and now women) know their places and can express and work out their frustrations within a protective organizational framework. What they need to know for survival, they learn from leaders tasked to look out for their welfare. Every person becomes an integral part of a team, and teams make it together—whether an eleven-man infantry squad or an international joint force of 500,000. But, of course, team members have to tuck part of their soul away to get the job done, and therein lies the corporate danger: a loss of soul, a narrowing of the range of consciousness.

The West Pointer in me yearned for more community than Harvard afforded, and I saw signs of yearning all around me. But leaders there—bound as they are to notions of fierce individualism and the libertarian's idea of freedom without restraint—

find it difficult to imagine how to create hierarchies that stabilize lives and generate synergy while still preserving people's right to their own ideas and their own way of doing things. Few at Harvard can imagine that a man or woman's way of doing things need not mean doing it alone. There was one other complication: To challenge a leader's ideas at Harvard was to challenge the person. Within that loose federation of brilliant individuals, I did not find a free and open marketplace of ideas. I found instead that leaders clung desperately to their own ideas. But to be an effective leader in academe, and perhaps anywhere else, men and women must be able to suffer the loss of their own creation. They must be able to glimpse a satisfying beauty in the work that others create under their direction.

Once, in Vietnam, I stood in the aftermath of a battle and observed the carnage of war. I helped train the soldiers who won the battle, but I had played no part in the fighting itself. I flew to the scene in my helicopter after the fighting was over and saw the carnage and the satisfaction on the soldiers' faces. Being there during the battle was not my job. My work had been done long before, and the satisfaction came to me privately as I stood watching those soldiers recover through the saving rituals they performed together—identifying and preserving the enemy's dead, policing the battlefield, stacking ammunition, burning left-over powder bags, hauling trash, shaving, drinking coffee, washing, talking—as they restored order and looked out for one another's welfare. They were bound up in what my friend Roy Reed calls the "throngs of community," and that communal satisfaction was its own pure reward for all of us.

I left Harvard out of frustration. I had gone there to fence myself off from my managerial urges and to test my mind while tasting that unfettered freedom West Point knew so little about. During the four years I spent there, I found my mind to be just fine, but Harvard sucked my spirit dry and gave me little return on my organizational investment. I found that I not only needed the stability that hierarchies afford, I wanted to be a part of an organization that gave me ownership. Everyone I taught with was yearning for ownership. People wanted to invest themselves; they wanted to belong. When I arrived at NYU just four months ago as the director of the expository writing program, I was, for the first time in almost twenty years, charged with sole responsibility for running an organization. Our product, to borrow your language, is a well-developed human mind—2,500 human minds each year, to be exact. Our major teaching tasks include creative thinking, critical reading, and clear writing. We even aim to impart a touch of elegance by the end of the required two-semester writing sequence, hoping that our students will write essays someone besides their mothers will want to read.

Our faculty are full-time graduate students who teach from fifteen to thirty students each term and earn a maximum salary of $9,000 plus tuition assistance. Each teacher invests countless hours in educational sessions that are an integral part of faculty development. And yet they stand in line for these jobs. Enabling hierarchies have a lot to do with it.

When I moved into the program, there had been a series of substitute directors for more than a decade. During that time, two women, who knew and understood something about the throngs of community, managed to preserve a program the university wanted to scrap because, in its view, NYU students weren't learning enough about how to write.

As it turned out, NYU had been right about the program's limitations and wrong about its value. But the two-semester sequence was neither systematic enough in its pedagogy nor clear enough about its aims. Nevertheless, the program itself had organizational strength and a life of its own, and I could see right away that my job was to preserve and supplement; it was not to destroy what was in place. The pedagogical problems would be easy to fix if only I could get inside the organization. Outside, positioned at the top, I would be ineffective. Against the university's constant pressure for change (and its inability to find a permanent director), the other directors, including the two women, had developed a siege mentality. When I arrived, they were hunkered down, a defensive within a self-inscribed protective circle. As an outsider with a military background, I walked in looking like a bad dream.

The organization itself resembled a truncated cone with three rings of responsibility separated by only a smidgen of hierarchy: at the top, five directors (each with an important functional responsibility and a protective sense of ownership for the whole program); on the second level, twelve mentors (third-year graduate assistants selected to help lead and develop the rest of the faculty); and at the base of the cone, more than a hundred graduate assistants—all committed to the task of preparing those 2,500 freshmen for their work in the university. The essential rhythms in this organization moved up and down the cone, around, and down and up, pulling the rings together, diminishing the hierarchical distance between them. There was a force field of involvement. Yet there seemed to be respect for hierarchical differences.

What I heard most often during my initial conversations with the teachers was a desire for more direction. But the plea was not for rules; it was for direction with space around it for individual variation. These were, after all, bright graduate students with notions of their own about unfettered freedom.

I had been working for years on what I call progressions—a series of connected assignments that move students in the direction of essays. Initially they were designed to keep students from trying to do everything the night before the paper was due; they became much more complex as I worked out ways to help students understand how to move from evidence to ideas to essays.

To satisfy the faculty's expressed need for direction and my own need for more definition in the program, I began to wed the notion of progressions to a new notion that came to me while reading Margaret Wheatley's book, *Leadership and the New Science*. Wheatley suggests that the best organizations have a "fractal quality." Within such organizations, defining characteristics of behavior repeat themselves endlessly, but there is infinite variety in the repetitions. Another way of getting at this factal notion is to say that organizational guideposts—what I'm now calling simple, elegant stems—provide a reference for self-reflexiveness; properly understood, these stems also set people free to do their jobs creatively.

In our work at NYU, we're discovering that even the complex tasks we teach day in and day out have a fractal quality. If we can identify the simple, elegant stem that repeats itself in each of these complex tasks that characterize our work, we get a much clearer sense of what we're doing without having to pre-scribe for our teachers just exactly how to do it. A stem provides direction with space around it.

An essay's stem, for example, suggests both form—a com-position with a beginning, middle, and ending—and function, a composition that develops an idea. An essay is a form that func-tions in a particular way. That simple stem accounts for all the essays ever written, but it sets a writer free to create an essay different from any ever written before, just as it sets a teacher free to create a pedagogy that will move students in the direc-tion of particular kinds of essays without prescribing for them just what such essays will turn out to be. Stems produce an effect like good hierarchies; they bind people together in joint enter-prises, creating intellectual involvement and discovery while providing freedom as well as direction.

Just a couple of weeks ago, sitting around the roundtable at the director's meeting, we began identifying a stem that ac-counts for our second-semester composition course. After much discussion and exploration, I had a try at finding words to ac-count for what we discovered together. Later, the other directors took on the task of revising. Working in pairs and then re-aligning the pairs for even more revision, we developed, over two days, a talking paper that gives next semester's work direc-tion but also leads to reappraisals of the first semester's work.

When we finished the document, it went out from the five directors, not from me. It went out as a talking paper, not as fixed policy. Already, we have had more than 20 sets of discus-sions with mentors and teachers. And even though the stem will eventually cause every teacher in the program to reappraise and perhaps redesign his or her writing course, we have not been managing contention during these discussions. We have been creating understanding. Revisions will surely follow. They must if we are serious about joint ownership.

Sitting there at that roundtable week after week, I am keenly aware that I must remain forever a bit of an outsider in that circle. My sense of direction—the stem that I help create—must be shaped from within the circle, but it must also be shaped by the university's needs, even if the university cannot specify them. No one else around that table except me need worry much about the university. But that obligation to look outside as well as within the circle reminds me that I have joint ownership in what I might have called 30 years ago, "my program, my command." Now, I know better than to claim such exclusive ownership, know that if the organization, any organization, is to maximize its effectiveness, there can be no false hierarchies within it. Enabling hierarchies bind committed people together in organizational communities while providing direction with space around it. They grant ownership and create obligations. And, unless I'm mistaken, they make people happy to come to work.

Appendix C

Toshiba's Research and Development Organization

At Toshiba, R&D is the responsibility of the Corporate Technology Strategy Committee chaired by Toshiba's senior technology executive. This activity reports to the CEO. The corporate track consists of the corporate R&D center and four other bodies. The corporate R&D center is made up of a group of ten central laboratories and one specialized department, each with about 100 scientists. The total staffing of this group is about 1,200 scientists and 200 technicians. On the corporate track there are, in addition to the corporate R&D center laboratories, three additional laboratories—Environmental Engineering, Manufacturing Engineering, and Systems Software Engineering—and one research center, the ULSI Research Center. One of the ten central labs is the Advanced Research Lab, which is almost totally centrally funded and where the focus is intended to wander to the bright blue sky.

The activities of these corporate track laboratories are separated from the immediate technical needs of the business groups and divisions. Their activities focus on a horizon of five to 10 years, and, with the exception of the Advanced Research Laboratory, are at least 50 percent contract funded by the business operations. One senior member of each of the corporate R&D center laboratories constitutes the Planning Council, responsible for continuous day-to-day contact between the business operations and the laboratories.

Immediately below are the group track, advanced development laboratories. Within Toshiba there are ten of these laboratories, which support the 11 business groups into which Toshiba's operations are organized. With the exception of the

Communications Systems and Technology Lab, which supports both the Information Equipment and Automation Systems Group and the Electronics and Telecom Systems Group, each of these development laboratories is linked to a single business group. Some labs, like the New Material Engineering Laboratory, while directly supporting the Materials and Components Group, have close links to the Industrial Equipment Group.

These labs are entirely funded by the business groups they support, and their advanced development programs are decided together with these business groups. These laboratories, however, report to the corporate Technology Strategy Committee, to which the corporate R&D center laboratories also report. The Technology Strategy Committee is chaired by Toshiba's senior technology executive and includes as its members the chief engineers of each group development laboratory as well as the director of the Corporate Technology Staff and the director of Corporate Laboratories.

The mission of these development laboratories is to think out, with the group, the future of each product line or family over a time horizon extending for five years. Their programs directly support business objectives over this intermediate term. They will develop technologies and make prototypes that serve as trial models of potential new products for the groups they support.

Within this R&D continuum, the development of a product or technology may take a course that can be quite different from that in a U.S. company. On the corporate track there is responsibility for market research as well as development and basic design trials. The development activities on this track focus on basic technologies, materials, and components. "Technology parcels" may be demonstrated. Samples of materials or components made within the corporate laboratories will be evaluated by internal customers. Occasionally an external customer may be sampled, depending on the nature of the material or component being developed.

The corporate Planning Council, made up of the heads of the 11 corporate R&D center laboratories, has its own market research responsibility. It has direct access to the market and will contact both internal and external end users. When a technology is transferred from the corporate to a group track, the transfer will not be of the technology alone but will usually include several members of the corporate R&D staff who may be transferred to the development laboratories for a period of from one to four years. Technology transfers from the group to the business unit track may be similarly accompanied by personnel. This method of transfer through people, rather than by data packages alone, is significant in differentiating Japanese technology transfer from technology transfer in most U.S. corporations. Between these tracks personnel will more frequently be transferred for the length of time it takes to carry out the technology transfer and then return to their specialty. At the product development level, personnel will more often be transferred to the production department as the next step on their career paths.

Using the new component, material, or technology, group track laboratories at Toshiba may produce from a few to several hundred prototypes or trial models, demonstrating a variety of feature sets or designs. These prototypes will not use final circuitry or special LSI. At this stage, the models of new or improved products tested may be large and cumbersome prototypes. Their objective is to validate a design. It is the design approval test that is carried out at this time and usually will not include cost and final quality feature objectives.

These prototypes or models secure customer reactions and aid the division or business unit product development groups in making final decisions on whether the ideas should be carried further, on cost trade-offs, and on the features the final product should embody. The prototypes are intensely evaluated by both internal and external end users. If the prototype evaluation is successful, the characteristics of the final product are broadly established, and the product development project begins. Product development is led by the product planning, design, and development groups on the business unit track with the readily available support of corporate or group R&D personnel. It is on this track that customer quality requirements and feature sets are determined, final cost trade-offs are made, and quality approval tests are completed. At this stage the number and size of PCBs will be reduced and specially designed LSI introduced. Mass production equipment will be used to produce samples, and mass trial production runs will precede production start-up. It is at the mass trial stage that the final production bugs will be eliminated.

These characteristics of Toshiba's closely linked three-track R&D activity and spousal organization are broadly representative of Japan's leading innovators.

Appendix D

Supplier Relationships in Japan: Case Studies

Yokogawa-Hewlett-Packard, Ltd. (YHP)

YHP works in close partnership with its key suppliers in developing new products. A typical relationship starts by making a model internally and giving it to the plastic parts supplier. The supplier, in interactive discussion with YHP, adds its knowledge of cost trade-offs and responds with a redesigned part with lower cost and increased ease of manufacture. To extract the maximum benefit from its suppliers' skills and specialized areas of expertise and to use them as true extensions of its own product development teams, the parent company tries to achieve a tight performance specification but with minimum interference in how the specification is to be achieved. By giving maximum freedom to suppliers, YHP stretches their capabilities. Key suppliers participate in a high number of development team meetings, and occasionally a supplier engineer will work at YHP.

YHP's policy is not to intervene between the first-tier suppliers and the second- or third-tier suppliers. The responsibility of the first-tier supplier to manage the tiers beneath it must be clear and undivided. In this system, there are few openings for new suppliers. Those that do penetrate usually initiate the contact with YHP and may occasionally be accepted if they have a special expertise or if there is an opening. The relationships are based on high personal and corporate confidence, with only limited need for written confidentiality agreements. Though the relationships embody strong personal confidence, the individuals are the representatives of their companies; the confidence transcends the individual and becomes that of the corporation and the responsibility of all its members.

The product development teams usually determine the suppliers, subject to the approval of the quality assurance department. Initially, except on standard parts, the purchasing department is barely involved. Purchasing's role on custom parts is that of the coordinator; it coordinates delivery and initiates price renegotiation after a year. YHP, like most other companies we interviewed in Japan, prefers two sources if volume permits.

Alps

Alps is an important supplier of control panels, keyboards, and other components that provide the interface between the user and a machine, such as a copier. The company is an important supplier to all types of electronic and electrical equipment manufacturers, including Canon, Sony, and YHP. One of its areas of expertise is in ergonomics, the human engineering that determines the ease, comfort, and efficiency with which the user interacts with a computer, a television, or a medical instrument. Angle of vision, feel, and positioning of controls for intuitive understanding form part of Alps's particular expertise. It spends heavily on research in these domains and is a valued early participant in the product development projects of its customers.

Once a year, the entire Alps group holds a new-product show for its best customers. It demonstrates products or control panels incorporating new features and technologies and obtains customer feedback. Many Alps customers have similar shows for their best customers at the prototype stage. In turn, they feed back to Alps the inputs they receive from demonstrating these models to their customers. Once Alps initiates a project with its customer, one engineer is assigned full time to that activity. This engineer will attend many of the design team meetings at the customer's location.

Alps componentry is so important to the appearance and acceptance of its customers' products that it will typically be brought in to work as a participant in the product development project at the conclusion of the preconcept phase. A rough sketch of the product is provided to Alps and frequently to one competitor. Both evaluate the sketch and during initial discussions focus on feature versus cost trade-offs. After these discussions, one or both will make a design proposal for the control panels and the other components. The design will be developed together with the product development team; the first hand-made "for appearances only" mock-up or prototype is delivered with cost estimates. At this stage, the equipment maker will usually choose a single contender as its control panel supplier. Though the preference is for two suppliers, a single source is usually used if the cost of dual tooling gets too high. Competition during the early design stages benefits the customer, who has two sets of design proposals to evaluate. The losing contender will be paid its full costs incurred, including overhead absorption. Occasionally this selection may be delayed until the second prototype is submitted. It does not hurt, of course, to have an inside track through frequent "golf talk" or "fun talk" sessions.

Each stage of the design activity is quoted and charged with full overhead cost absorption, standard practice in both the commercial electronics and the consumer electronics industries. Thus, neither Alps nor its competitors incurs unrecovered costs if either fails to get the production order. Features are fixed at the prototype stage. Internal tests and some external tests are carried out by the client, the original equipment manufacturer (OEM), to identify possible problems and to see that end user needs are met. Alps does not attempt to see around the OEM in this regard but carries on extensive ergonomic research of its own. Work proceeds quickly. Alps engineers appear at the customer's site and participate in development team meetings as needed. Electronic linkage into the CAD systems of its customers may not be far off. Before the final design is approved, usually two successive handmade prototypes representing different stages of design development will be made. The final design may include additional modifications. No additional prototypes embody these final modifications. Production begins three to six months after approval.

Alps has three types of suppliers: for standard items (such

as resistors or condensers), custom items (such as plastic parts, printed circuit boards, harnesses, and metal parts), and small shops that specialize in handmade parts for prototypes. The relationships between them may be typified as "master-slave" rather than as the partnerships that typify the relationships between Alps and its customers. Alps assembles the prototype parts before submitting them to the customer. When the final design has been approved, tooling starts in earnest, with some done in-house and some done by suppliers that bid competitively to Alps specifications.

Alps maintains in-house technology for some of the more critical parts that it purchases. Some mold-making and plastic injection parts manufacturing is retained in-house, as well as all die-making and some metal parts stamping. Alps feels that without this internal knowledge, it would be unable to judge the level of technology coming from suppliers. It has confidentiality agreements with all of its suppliers, many of which supply components to Alps's competitors. Alps's procurement department handles negotiations with its suppliers. As in the case of the OEM, the product development engineers choose a supplier. When the design is approved, procurement puts it out for competitive bid.

Appendix E

NEC: A Commitment to Change

Kemp Dwenger

For ten years, I had the opportunity to participate with Dr. Koji Kobayashi, chairman of NEC, as a co-board member of a joint venture between NEC and GTE-Sylvania. The joint venture company was formed in 1972 to manufacture fluorescent lamps for the Japanese market on high-speed horizontal equipment, at that time proprietary to GTE-Sylvania. The venture was formed just as the first oil crisis turned the market growth rates negative for lamps in Japan and other industrialized countries. It was not a propitious time to start the joint venture, but it was a time with an immense, though wasted, learning opportunity.

For most of the ten-year life of the joint venture, Dr. Kobayashi, at the quarterly board meetings we both attended, implored the factory to reduce costs. At each board meeting, the manufacturing manager reported on the cost reductions accomplished and the targets for the next board meeting. This was the same period when most U.S. companies accepted manufacturing cost increases as long as they did not exceed the rate of inflation. This is the exact time when, in several industries, Japanese companies gained leadership over their U.S. competitors. Dr. Kobayashi saw the challenge and the opportunity. The joint venture, managed by NEC, became the most efficient fluorescent lamp manufacturing location in GTE-Sylvania's worldwide factory organization.

Well before GTE sold its shares to NEC in the early 1980s, the joint venture had attained materials efficiencies almost ten percentage points higher than those at GTE-Sylvania's other factories and had cut, in Japan, the change-over time to convert the production line from one lamp length to another from one full shift to 20 minutes. All of what we identify today as total quality management methodology was spread before us, but we failed to learn. At the end of the ten years, manufacturing efficiencies, continuously improving, were the best in the world, but the learning opportunity was lost on other GTE-Sylvania manufacturing locations, which saw the accomplishment as a threat rather than as an opportunity, and patterns of behavior failed to change.

Dr. Kobayashi challenged and established the credibility and urgency of the objective. Neither he nor anyone else from a staff or headquarters group attempted to tell the factory how to achieve the objective. They established what it was they had to do and did it. Dr. Kobayashi demonstrated that a leader at his very best may be an alchemist whose role it is to turn threat into challenge. Threat implies loss, and challenge implies opportunity; and a challenge is a threat that is perceived in time to do something about it.

Index

Abbaye de Villeneuve, 21
accountability, 42–47, 68
Ackoff, Russell, 19
affinity diagrams, 127, 130, 135
Airbus, 4–5
Akao, Yoji, 122
Allaire, Paul, 187–188
Alps, 225–227
Altmansberger, H.N., 168
American Airlines, 35
American Supplier Institute, 79
Analog Devices, 94, 97–98, 167
Apple Computer, 41, 109, 158
Astra Hassle, 52
AT&T, 109, 127–128, 175, 210

base pay, 162, 167
beliefs, 138
benchmarks, vii, 60
Berg Electronics, 76
Bertalanffy, Ludwig von, 15
best practices, xi, 57–60
Best Practices (Department of the Navy), 106
Bisone, Gian Carlo, 38
Black & Decker, 34–35, 52–53
blue sky projects, 149
Boeing, 4–5, 10, 16, 46, 73, 76, 210
    four-fields map in, 86–87
Bolman, Lee G., 191

Bose, 130, 131, 163
bottleneck engineering, 147–149
bottleneck technologies, identifying, 114
break-even time, 45
breakthroughs, 41
British Rover Group, 22, 70
Brown, John Seely, 188
Brown, Susan, 127–128
Bruck, Christian, 154
"brush-up" reviews, 107
budgetary decisions, 12
burnout, 14
business unit development, 142
Business Week, 4

Calsonic Llanilli Radiators, 97, 161
Canon, 110–111, 144
Carter, John, 102
cascading training programs, 78
Center for Quality Management, 78
Champy, James, 18
change, 185
    continuous, 187–193
    and product development, 192–193
    rippling effect of, 20
charter, 74–75, 99
    in four-fields map, 82
chat boxes, 180

Chiba, Genya, 149
chief executive officer, 190
Chrysler Corp., 22, 28, 72–73, 76, 77,
    152, 189–190, 197
circular pattern for organization,
    ix–x
Claflin, Bruce, 18
Clark, Kim B., ix
Clausing, Don, 125
Cohen, Lou, 126
Cohen, Susan, 167
collaboration, 174
    cross-organization, 65
collaboratories, 182
colocation, 76–78
communication, 15–16
    best practices, 58, 60
    between core firm and subcon-
        tractor, 155
    company-wide, x
    correlation with distance, 77–78
    electronic, 16
    horizontal, xi
    in Japan, 155–156
    across organizational boundaries,
        vii–viii
    real-time system, 179
    seamless, 50–54
    streamlining of, 41
Compaq, 42
compartmentalization, 28–29
competence centers, 30
competencies, emphasis on, 72
competition, 96, 97
competitive analysis, 120
concept engineering, 128–130
concurrent engineering, 44, 76
Condit, Phil, 10
conformance errors, 98
connectivity, 196
    model, 177–178
contextual inquiry, 130, 134–136

continuous change, 187–193
continuous disequilibrium, 20–21
continuous improvement, 98
contract funding, of corporate labs,
    144–145
control over decisions, 47–49
coordination, early, 45
core firm, communication with sub-
    contractor, 155
core group, 70
core technologies, identifying,
    145–147
Corning Company, 58, 168–170
corporate labs, contract funding of,
    144–145
corporate research, 141
Cray, 211
crisis management, 11, 12
cross-boundary communication, viii
cross-function management, 25
cross-organization collaboration, 65,
    195
cross-organization team, line man-
    agers as, 28
Csikszentmihalyi, Mihaly, 56
customer interviewing, 130, 132–134
customer needs
    communicating, 16
    problems defining, 8–9
customers
    in delivery team, 71–72
    direct contact with, 53
    prototype evaluation by, 142
    relation of core team to, 73
    satisfied, 24
    see also voice of customer
customized products, 42
Cusumano, Michael, ix
cycle times, speed of, 3
Cyrix, 11

Dartmouth College, Thayer School
    of Engineering, ix, 20

Data General, 158
Deal, Terrence E., 191
decisions
    control over, 47–49
    information accessibility and, 182
defect rate, 94
delivery teams, 70–74, 188
Deming, W. Edwards, 39
Denend, Les, 159–160
departmental approach to product
    development, 10
Department of Defense, 44
Department of the Navy, *Best Practices*, 106
derivative product, 42
design, first-time success rate, 6
design errors, 98
design reviews, 107, 108, 109–110,
    111, 112–113
development teams
    responsibilities of, 45
    sharing ownership on, 41
Digital Equipment Corporation, 43–
    44, 73, 126–127, 158
    4-fields technique in, 88, 90
Dimancescu, Dan, ix, x
Dion, Eric P., 173, 181
disequilibrium, continuous, 20–21
disposal of products, 47
distance, correlation with communication, 77–78
documenting system, in Toshiba, 49
do-loop principle, 3, 66, 197
Drucker, Peter, 24
Dwenger, Kemp, ix
dynamically stable organization,
    208–209
dynamic metrics, 101–103

Eastman Kodak, 93
EET Limited, 162
Eintracht, Fred, 166, 171

electronic communication, 16, 182
electronic information technology,
    46–47
enabling hierarchy, 26–28, 212–219
engagement teams, 35
engineering change orders, in NEC,
    113
engineering effort curves, 11
engineering prototype, 114
environmental laws, 47
equilibrium, 187
error rate, 98–99
    best practices to manage, 58
errors
    cost of correcting, 10
    in product development cycle,
        9–11
    risk of passing, 48
    tracking, 107
Europe, 197
    productivity statistics, 24
Evans, Roger, 187
exit criteria, 43
extended members, of product development team, 71
external sourcing, 153

face-to-face contact, 76–78
Federal Aviation Administration, 5,
    46
Federal Express, 21, 78, 180
federalism, 205
Fisher, Anne, 189
Fisher, George, 93
$5 \times$ to $10 \times$ improvements, 93, 99
focus groups, 134
Ford Motor Company, 21, 78, 125
    Rouge plant, 153
    Team Taurus, ix, 28, 70
four-fields mapping, 60, 80–90, 106
    elements in, 82, 84
Frank, Allan, 179–180

Fujimoto, Takahiro, ix
Fujitsu, 102–103
Fuji-Xerox, 109, 115–118
functions, role of, 32–33
"fun talk," 155
Furukawa, Osamu, 148
"fuzzy after launch," 46
"fuzzy front end," 45

Gage, Stan, 30
Gardner, Glenn, 190
Garvin, David, ix
gate reviews, 117
gating decision points, 47
Genentech, 211
General Electric, 189
General Motors, 28, 38, 154
global information systems, 21
goals, into action, 192
goal sharing, 168
"golf talk," 155
Goodyear Tire & Rubber, 53
government agencies, as customers,
    73–74
group development, 142
group skills, training in, 78–79
groupware, 181
guidelines, in four-fields map, 82

half-life metrics, 94–98, 146
    applying to product develop-
    ment, 98–101
Hammer, Michael, 18
Hanna, David P., 35
Hayes, Robert H., ix
Heidrik, Buck, 195
Hellman, Wayne, 170–171
Hess, George, 176–177
Hewlett-Packard, 8, 26, 30–32, 44–
    45, 58, 66, 195
    process hierarchy, 31–32
    product definition at, 120

hierarchical control, 3
hierarchy, 197
    changeover to holistic structure,
    29–36
    enabling, 26–27, 212–219
    flattening, 188
Hill, Will, 34, 35
Hines, Peter, 153, 161
Hjort, Hans, 74–75, 128
Hoffman-LaRoche, 210
holistic organization, 19, 21, 195
    determining extent of, 23
    hierarchical structure changeover
    to, 29–36
    management, 20
Honda, 42
horizontal communication, xi
horizontal management, 30
horizontal processes, 26, 57
horizontal systems, 209
horizontal teams, 26
Howie, Tom, 162
Hoy, Patrick, 21

IAPD (International Association for
    Product Development), x, xi, 6,
    57–58
IBM Corporation, 18–19, 41, 158,
    210
incremental product development,
    41–42
infinitely flat organization, 207–208
information, real-time exchange, 46
information accessibility, in product
    development, 174
information processing model,
    199–201
information sharing, xi, 50–54
    training, 78–79
Information Systems Group,
    102–103
information technology, and orga-
    nizational models, 207–209

Ingersoll Milling Machine Company, 176
innovation, 140
   in organizations, 210–211
Institute for Defense Analyses, 76
Institute for the Future (Palo Alto), 177, 182
integrated approach to development process, 48
Intel, 11, 114
interference, management by, 11–12, 40
International Association for Product Development (IAPD), x, xi, 6, 57–58

Japan, 22, 80–81, 189, 197
   communication in, 53, 155–156
   management in, ix-x
   product development in, 4
   productivity statistics, 24
   strategic process teams in, 68
   supplier relationships in, 224–227
   vertical aggregation, 153–157
Japanese model for mastering organizational complexity, 24
Japan Systems Corporation, 125
Johansen, Robert, 177
Juenz, Bela, 141
Juki, 124–125
just-in-time methods, 156

Kano, Noriako, 136
Kano diagram, 137
Kano method, 130
Katayama, Yoshiaki, 125
Katayama, Zenzaburo, 61
Katzenbach, Jon R., *The Wisdom of Teams*, 66–67
Kerr, Steve, 165
Kidder, Tracy, *The Soul of a New Machine*, 14

Kiesler, Sara, 182
Kimberly-Clark, 135
KJ method, 130
Kleeman, Michael, 73, 88
knowledge, purpose of, 175
knowledge management, 173–183
Knowledge Manager, 180–181
Kobayashi, Koji, 228–229
Komatsu, 58, 60
KPMG-Peat Marwick, 179
Kurogane, Kenji, 25
Kyocera, 211

language, establishing common, 88, 90
Lasker, Harry, 181
latent needs, 136–137, 144
lateral organization, 1
lateral teaming hierarchy, 27
lattice organization, 209
Lawler, Edward, 53
Leadership and the New Science (Wheatley), 173, 217
lead users, 134
   feedback from, 119
Lee, Chris, 22, 71
legacy systems, 175
Levi Strauss, 21, 177
line managers, 28
line people, team management by, x
local area networks, 173–174
Longworth, George, 161
Lotus, 44, 167–168, 170
Lucasfilm, 182

The Machine That Changed the World, ix, 24
Machine Theory, 35
macrolevel network forms, 202–203
Malone, Thomas, 182

management, 191
  cross-function, 25
  new system of, 25–26
management by interference, 11–12,
    40
  avoiding, 58
management reviews, 107, 108–109
marketing, 24
master-slave relationships, 163
Matsushita, 210
McCracken, Edward, 159
McDonough, Kevin, 11
McNealy, Scott, 159
McQuarrie, Edward, 132, 133
Meadows, D. L., 198
measurement, 91–92
  need to recalibrate, 104
mentors, 40
Merck, 210
merit pay, 162
metrics, 91–105, 167, 196
  dynamic, 101–103
  half-life, 95–97
  limitations of, 103–104
  motivational, 93–101
  vs. measurement, 91–92
Meyer, Arnoud de, viii
milestones, in four-fields map, 82
Milliken, 26
Minato, T., 155
Mitel, 76, 90
Mohrman, Susan Albers, 61
Morone, Joseph, 140
Morris, Paul, 161
motivation, 62
  critical inhibitors of, 64
  variable pay and, 167
motivational metrics, 93–101
Motorola, 41, 189

NASA, 106
National Semiconductor, 51

NEC, 147, 228–229
  Yonazawa laptop plant, 111, 143
NEC-NIMs, 5–6, 108, 124
needs, communication by team,
    86–87
network organizations, 202–207
Nippon Denso, 99

objectives, reward systems and, 172
open-ended questions, for customer
    interview, 133
opportunity cost, 45
optimal experience, 55
organization
  optimum size of, 15
  spousal form of, 149
organizational complexity, 24
organizational models, 199–211
  architectural trends, 201
  information processing model,
    199–201
  information technology and,
    207–209
  innovative, 210–211
  networks, 202–207
organization architecture, 188
organization chart, teaming, 33–34
outsourcing, Western trend in, 158
overlapping project cycles, 11
ownership, sharing on development
    teams, 41

Parikh, Yogesh, 134
partner associations, 156
patent reviews, 110–111
Patterson, Marvin L., 36, 194
pay at risk, 167
performance gaps, 97, 146, 167
  size and time frame for, 99
perfomance measurement, 91
Pitney Bowes, 175–176

plan-do-check-act spiral, 39
  on four-fields map, 82
Polaroid, 51
PowerPC, 41
predictive measures, 102
prioritization, 13, 147
problem anticipation rate, 101
process-focused management,
  30–32
process teams, value of, 36
Procter & Gamble, 21, 26, 46, 73, 128
product definition, 119–138
  quality function deployment,
    122–128
product development, 38–54
  applying half-life metrics to,
    98–101
  benchmarking, vii
  change and, 192–193
  incremental, 41–42
  problems in, 6–17
  repetition in, 6
  rewards and, 170
  success in, 3–4
  systemic span of, 194
  in Toshiba, 49
  of world-class performers, 39
product development cycle
  earliest stages of, 43
  errors in, 9–11
  overlapping, 11
  span of activities in, 43
  speed in managing, 4
  stages, 59
productivity comparisons, Japan,
  U.S., and Europe, 24
productivity evaluation, 114
product lives, 38
product reviews, 114
projects
  failure or success of, 120–121
  number of, 12–13

prototypes, 114, 142

qualitative approach to best practice
    identification, 57
quality assurance chart, 81
quality function deployment,
    122–128
quality reviews, 110
quality tables, 107, 122, 123, 129, 148
questionnaires, 134
Quinn, James Brian, 141, 158

R&D
  Japanese continuum, 141–144
  organization in Toshiba, 220–223
  spending on, 141, 145
R&D strategy, vs. business strategy,
    144–145
Raychem, 211
Raytheon Corporation, 99
real-time information exchange, 46,
    179
regional aggregation, 160
regulations, in four-fields map, 82
regulatory agencies, 46
Renaissance Strategy Group, 181
resources management, 194
results-focused measures, 92
reviews, 106–118
  in Canon, 110–111
  design, 107, 108, 109–110, 111,
    112–113
  management, 107, 108–109
  methods of, 108–109
  patent, 110–111
  product, 114
  quality, 110
  technology, 110
  in Toshiba, 50
rewards, 165–172, 197
  for teams, 166
rework, 9

Rockart, John, 182
Rockwell International, 126
root cause analysis, 99
Russell, Peter, 187

Saab Automotive AB, 7
Sabre Development Systems, 35
Schmidt, Al, 175–176
Schneiderman, Art, 91, 94, 146
Schrage, Michael, 175
scientists, 185
Scott, Michael, 158
senior management, 65–66, 192
    involvement in reviews, 117
    as mentors, 40
senior process teams, 66, 67–70, 188
sequential phases, 48
shamrock organizations, 204–205
Silicon Graphics, 159
Silicon Valley, 21, 157–160
skills, paying for acquisition of, 167
software tools, for quality function
    deployment, 126
Sony, 42, 146
The Soul of a New Machine (Kidder),
    14
span of activity, 41
spider's web network organization,
    203–204
spot awards, 170
spousal form of organization, 149
Sproull, Lee, 182
starburst organizations, 204
star diagrams, 128
static measures, 92
statistical justification, of best prac-
    tices, 57
statistical process control charts, 101
Ste. Suisse Microélectronique et
    d'Horlogerie, 138
Stotz, Roger, 162, 172
strategic core processes, x

strategic processes, 27–28
strategic process management, xi
strategic process teams, 188
strategy, 194
subcontractor, communication with
    core firm, 155
success, first-time rate in design, 6
Sun Microsystems, 159
supplier associations, 161
supplier networks, 196
    purposes of, 156–157
suppliers, 152–163
    in delivery team, 71–72
    partnerships with, 162–163
    relationships in Japan, 224–227
system needs, individual perform-
    ance and, 19
systems of scope, 209

tasks, in four-fields map, 82
teaming organization chart, 33–34
team members, in four-fields map,
    82
teams, 61–79
    accountability, 42–47
    engagement, 35
    horizontal, 26
    important characteristics, 67–79
    management by line people, x
    rewards for, 166
    tiers of, 188–189
    understanding, 62–67
technology management, 140–150,
    196
    organizational links, 149–150
technology reviews, 110
telephone interviews, 134
terminology, gaining agreement on,
    88, 90
Texas Instruments, 171–172
Textron Defense, 170–171
Thermo Electron, 211

3M, 211
T-matrix, 107
Toshiba, 47–49
  documenting system, 49
  product development process, 49
  research and development,
    220–223
  spousal form of organization, 149
  testing and review system, 50
Toyota, 25, 58, 60, 119, 143, 153–154
  supplier responsibility, 157
training, 78–79
Trane Company, four-fields technique in, 87–88
transactional logistics, 174
transitional states, 21
tree diagrams, 130
Tsuda, Yoshi, 80
Turner, Dennis, 161

Uchimaru, Kiyoshi, 106, 124
Uenohara, Michiyuki, 104, 142
United States, productivity statistics, 24
user needs, best practices, 58
user requirement errors, 98

Veraldi, Lewis, ix
vertical aggregation, 153–157
vertical disaggregation, 153, 157–160
vertical systems, 209
voice of customer, 123
  capturing, 119
  classifying statements, 136
  emerging practices, 137–138

gathering, 127
  translating into products,
    128–138
Volvo, 75, 128

Waldrop, M. Mitchell, 185
Wales, 160
Wal-Mart, 73, 180
Weisbord, Marvin, 18
Welch, Jack, 189
Welsh Development Agency, 160
Wheatley, Margaret, *Leadership and
  the New Science*, 52, 173, 217
Wheelwright, Steven C., ix, 65
Whirlpool Corporation, 152
Wilson, Edith, 8, 120–121
W.L. Gore and Associates, 209
Womack, J., 74
workplace complexity, 22
workthrough, 108
world-class performers, 21
  product development process of,
    39
  systemic response to problems,
    195

Xerox, 78, 187–188
Xerox/InterMatrix benchmarking
  study, vii, x

Yamanouchi, Teruo, 110, 111
Yokogawa-Hewlett-Packard, Ltd.,
  95, 224–225

Zaltman, Gerald, 138